BANGLA GASTRONOMY

THE JOURNEY OF BENGALI FOOD

ANANYA BANERJEE

Popular Prakashan
www.popularprakashan.com

Published by Harsha Bhatkal
for Popular Prakashan Pvt. Ltd.
301, Mahalaxmi Chambers
22, Bhulabhai Desai Road
Mumbai 400026
www.popularprakashan.com

First Published 2018

(4492)
ISBN: 978-81-7991-933-0

Photography: Sanjit Sen (cover), Arindam Basu (back flap)
Food Photography: Ananya Banerjee, Arijit Biswas
Food Styling: Ananya Banerjee
Sketches: Ananya Banerjee
Design: Anjali Sawant

PRINTED IN INDIA
By Saurabh Printers (P) Ltd.
Plot No. 67, A-68, Ecotech, Ext. I
Kasna, Greater Noida-201306 (UP)

RAVE REVIEWS

Bangla Gastronomy - The Journey of Bengali Food by Ananya Banerjee takes us through the various influences on Bengali food like Mughlai, Chinese, Anglo-Indian, and British as well as the traditional Bengali food we eat today! A very interesting read, indeed!

—Sanjeev Kapoor, Chef Extraordinaire, Padma Shri Awardee, Entrepreneur, Author, TV Anchor

A cookbook with nice stories, authentic recipes and cooking made easy for you and me.

—Arnab Goswami, Managing Director, Editor-in-Chief, Co-Founder, Republic TV

Bangla-ranna (Bengali cooking) is the ultimate expression of love and respect. When I try Ananya's recipes that is what I find.

—Ranveer Brar, Celebrity Chef, Master Chef Judge & Anchor Chef, Living Foodz

Exciting, knowledgeable and edgy. 50 shades of real good cooking. It's a Bomb!

—Vicky Ratnani, Anchor Chef, FoodFood & Living Foodz

As a food professional I am always exploring the new and delicious. This book is definitely a work of culinary art that will have a permanent place in my collection of favorite cookbooks.

—Anirudhya Roy, Executive Chef, Taj Lands End

Completely BONGED over by the recipes . . . It's a must have for my kitchen library.

—Shailendra Kekade, Anchor Chef, FoodFood

If you want to discover the heart of any Bengali, this book is where you should start.

—Kunal Vijayakar, Food Writer & TV Anchor

Ananya's ability to cook beautiful food is matched only by her interest in the history and origins of the recipe. This book is a testament to both her passions.

—Antoine Lewis, Food & Wine Writer, Host, 94.3 Radio One

Having eaten some of the lovely Bengali food that Ananya cooks, I am glad that she has written this book.

—Kalyan Karmakar, Author, Food Columnist & Blogger

I have tried a few of her recipes from this book and compared it to the other Bengali culinary treats and Ananya wins hands down!

—Mahesh Thakur, Film & TV Actor

The globalisation of Bengali food is depicted in this book beautifully.

—Aniruddha Roy Chowdhury, Film Director

Amazing cook book with authenticity. I would say recipes with soul, without losing authenticity.

– Gopi Nandakumar, Executive Chef,
Hyatt Regency Mumbai

She cooks with effortless ease...almost like her paintings and the variety and repertoire makes me spellbound. I wish her great success with her book, which I am sure will touch many with her heartwarming food!

—Chef Saby (Sabyasachi Gorai),
Celebrity Chef & Restaurateur

Well-known culinary artiste Ananya cooks up a storm, superbly capturing the myriad flavours of Bengal's vast gastronomic repertoire . . . this is a must buy for budding cooks and experts alike.

—Pritha Sen, Food Historian & acclaimed Author

AUTHOR'S NOTE

When Bengalis get together, the conversation will usually revolve around food, football and politics – with eatables taking precedence.

When you talk about Bengali cuisine, what crops up in most non-Bengali minds is fish and rice (*maach-bhaat* as it is known in Bengal). But it is not as fishy as you think! A fabulous vegetarian spread and an amazing range of sweets are also hallmarks of Bengali cuisine.

Bengalis, like the French, spend not only a great deal of time thinking about food but also in its preparation and eating. Quips like "Bengalis live to eat" and "Bengalis spend most of their income on food" are not misplaced. The early morning shopping for fresh vegetables and fish, is the prerogative of the head of the family, and it is believed that he alone can pick the best at a bargain.

Nothing fishy about fish

Nature has blessed Bengal abundantly with countless rivers, ponds and lakes. Fresh sweet water fish is one of the most distinctive features of Bangla cuisine. Unending varieties of fish like *rui, katla, koi, pabda* and the queen of fish *ilish*, draws Bengalis towards their innate pride-catch. Prawns, shrimp and crabs are also in abundance. Most Bengal villages have multiple ponds, usually used for pisciculture. At least one meal with the celebrated *maach-bhaat* is a reality in most Bengali homes, on most days.

Vegetarian Bengalis – not so uncommon

Contrary to popular impression, Bengalis excel in cooking regional vegetables. Nothing goes wasted in their kitchen. Vegetable peels, stalks and leaves are judiciously used to prepare delicacies.

The influence of 'widow-food' has given rise to *niramish* or vegetarian food in Bengali cuisine. Widows of Bengal led a very restrictive monastery life till some years ago. Not only were they barred from having any non-vegetarian items, but they also did not use onion-garlic in their food. In short, any food that created heat in the body was banned – resulting in a new type of tasty vegetarian cuisine.

Sweet tooth

Bengalis are known to have a sweet tooth. In a typical Bengal city, every tenth shop will probably be a sweetmeat shop. I often wonder whether diabetes has by-passed the Bengalis!

The Portuguese taught Bengal the art of *chhena* making. The fresh cheese they prepared is nothing but *queso-fresco* or cottage cheese (*chhena*), with which most Bengali sweets are made. While the rest of India considered '*chhena*' as inauspicious being made out spoilt milk, but Bengal taught the rest how the same can be converted to create the world beating delicacies - the Bengali sweets.

Grandmother's sweets

In the yester-years, our grand moms, who usually stayed back at homes, experimented a lot with their cuisine - usually the sweet variety. Some mouth-watering examples are: *pithe-puli*, home-made sweets - pan-fried, steamed or boiled, especially made during the harvest festival; *bhapa* (steamed) *pithe* and *bhaja* (fried) *pithe* to name a few.

Cooking techniques

Bengal's distinct cooking techniques sets the cuisine aside from any other. The ingredients keep varying, but the cooking method remains the same under some broad categories. To cite an example, "*jhol*" is a light, watery concoction, cooked almost daily in a Bengali home. It can be made with vegetables (*niramish-jhol*), fish (*macher-jhol*) or meat (*mangshor jhol*). To take another instance, "*chechki*", is a lightly spiced stir-fried preparation tempered with '*panch phoron*'. It could be '*alu* (potato)-*chechki*' or '*kopi* (cauliflower)-*chechki*'. The variety is just never-ending. Each one provides a distinctive style, taste and flavour, and is undoubtedly delectable and tasty.

Food for all occasions

From birth to death, Bengali food rises to every occasion.

When the newborn tastes solid food for the first time called **'mukhe-bhaat'**, the celebration sees an ample use of rice cooked in various forms like - payesh or kheer, ghee bhaat or pulao.

The Bengali wedding or ***'biye-bari'*** is another event to flaunt culinary delights. Everything, from intricate fish preparations to mouth-watering sweetmeat varieties are served.

Jamai shoshti is the day to pamper and welcome the son-in-law and of course, impress him. Extravagant and elaborate dishes are usually made, like '*kobiraji-cutlet*' and '*golda-chingri malai-curry*'.

The Anglo-Indian influence has made Kolkata and other towns in Bengal celebrate ***Christmas*** with much gusto, serving roasts, cakes and bakes. ***Poush-sankranti*** is celebrated with the onset of the harvest season with *pithe, puli* and *pathi-shapta* (traditional sweets) prepared usually with ground freshly harvested rice, *nolen-gur* or fresh jaggery and scraped coconut.

Aai-buro-bhaat, the last bachelor meal of the bride and groom-to-be, is served with a variety of delicacies. ***Shaad***, the meal celebrating a new pregnancy is usually served with impressive fish preparations so that the expectant mother receives loads of protein. And finally, ***sradhho***, a spread dedicated to the departed soul - a send-off meal that contain items especially liked by the departed soul.

Order of serving food

Bengalis are very particular about the sequence or the order in which food should be served. Each dish is to be had separately with a little rice so that the individual flavours can be enjoyed.

Generally, a 'lunch' would follow the following order: the first item served with a little *ghee*, poured over a small portion of rice and eaten with a pinch of salt. Then comes the bitter preparation *shukto*, followed by lentils or *daal*, served with roasted or fried vegetables (*bhaja or bharta*).

Next arrives the vegetable dishes - the lightly spiced *chenchki* and *chokka*, followed by the heavily spiced *dalna* and *ghonto*, some of which are cooked with fish. Then it is the turn of *jhol* and *jhal*, generally made with fish.

Chicken or mutton preparations come next, provided it is on the menu for the day. *Chaatni* served with crisp savoury wafers, called *papod* comes in next to clear the palate.

You would be spoilt for choice when it comes to desserts in a Bengali meal. The legendary *rosogolla, sondesh* and *mishti-doi* can all be served in ample portions.

The meal is finally concluded with the handing out of betel-leaf (*paan*), which is considered not only to aid digestion but serve as a mouth freshener too. A well-digested meal after all makes for a very satisfying meal experience!

Served in style

A traditional meal is eaten seated on the floor. Small, individual carpets called *ason*, is spread for each person to sit on and the meal is served on a large gun-metal or silver plate (*thala*) or banana leaf (*kola-pata*).

Various food items are placed in bowls (*batis*) around the top of the *thala or kola-pata*, running from right to left. Rice is mounded and placed in the middle, with a little salt, chilli and a lemon slice placed on the upper right hand corner. Fingers of the right hand are used and strict etiquette is observed with regard to this.

Modern times have done away with many of these rituals with commercial caterers serving food on dishes or plates of various sizes to guests seated at tables and chairs. Bengalis however still prefer to use their hands to have the delectable servings.

Influences

Bengali cuisine as we see it today is a result of different culinary influences from all those who had established their base in undivided Bengal over the course of time. The major influences on Bengali cuisine have been the Mughals, British, Anglo-Indians, Chinese and of course, the traditional Hindus.

Mughlai influence

Murshidabad, which is now in West Bengal, and Dhaka the capital of Bangladesh (erstwhile East Bengal), used to be the capital of the Nawab of Bengal during the Mughal rule. Rich sauces and meat preparations were introduced during this era. Various kebabs of whole lamb (*mussallaum*) came into being.

When the British attacked India, Tipu Sultan of Mysore and Nawab Wajid Ali Khan from Awadh (now Lucknow) exiled after their defeat, took refuge in Kolkata. Both the Nawabs especially the Awadhi Nawab brought along hundreds of *bawarchis* (cooks) and *mashalchis* (spice-makers). The *Mughlai* food found in Bengal is the result of this exodus. Enchanting dishes like *chaap* (ribs slow-cooked on a *tawa*), *rezala* (meat cooked in thin yogurt and cardamom gravy) and the signature Bengal *biriyani*, which is distinctly different from the rest of the country, put its stamp on Bengal's culinary map.

Kathi-roll of Bengal, is a famous Mughlai influenced dish. The mutton and chicken rolls spiced with fresh lemon juice, finely chopped green chillies, red onions and salt rolled in an eggy *paratha*, are simply mouth-watering!

Raj influence gentry

English and Jewish bakers such as Flury's and Nahoum's, dominated the confectionery industry. They ensured a migration of dishes from British tables to everyday Bengali homes, resulting in unique creations such as *pêṭis* (savory turnovers, derived from the English "patties").

Another enduring contribution to Bengali cuisine is *pau-ruṭi* or Western-style bread. The Raj-era cuisine lives on, especially in the variety of finger foods popularised in the 'pucca' clubs of Kolkata, such as *mutton chop, kabiraji-cutlet* or *fish-orly*.

The British also influenced food in a somewhat different way. Many British families in India hired cooks, and through them discovered local food in a cross migration of flavours. The cuisine had to be toned down or modified to suit the tastes of the English begums or *'mem-sahibs'*.

The most distinct influence is seen in the desserts, many of which were created specifically to satisfy the British - most notably the very popular sweet *leđikeni* named after the first Vicereine Lady Canning - it is a derivative of the *'pantua'* created especially for an event hosted by her.

Anglo-Indian influenced tasty-bites

Kolkata, the capital of West Bengal houses typical Anglo-Indian food. This is not purely the influence of the British. Bengal was once the home of a French colony, and also hosted the Portuguese, Dutch and other Europeans. These collective Western influences are seen in the food created to satisfy the tastes of the erstwhile western rulers.

The result is a unique cuisine. Local ingredients adapted to French and Italian cooking techniques—characterised by creamy sauces, the restrained use of spices and new techniques such as baking. To cite a few examples, *makallah* (Jewish), *soufflé* and *ala-kiev* (French), and *vindaloo* (Portuguese), are tasty additions to the table.

Chinese influenced hunger-clinchers

In the late 18th century, immigrants from China settled in Bengal in large numbers. The birth of *sweet-corn soup, chilli-chicken* and *chowmein* happened. *Chopsuey* became a favourite and versions like *American Chopsuey* and *Chinese Chopsuey* got talked about. Chinese-influenced food discussions cannot be complete without the mention of the ever popular Calcutta-Chinese or 'Tangra-Chinese'. It is located on the eastern by-pass region of Kolkata, where most of the Chinese settled and formed the 'Chinatown'.

When a large number of Tibetans migrated into Indian Territory, following the 14th Dalai Lama's flight from China, they brought with them their own delicacies to add to this genre. Like the very popular *momo* (a kind of dumpling) or *thukpa* (a hearty noodle soup), to name a few. Tibetans and Nepali immigrants also found ready employment in the Bengal-kitchens as 'Chinese' cooks because of their looks. They helped power thousands of eateries that serve this unique fusion, on virtually every street corner in Kolkata.

Unending range

We live in a country where the recipe keeps changing every few kilometres. New ingredients are added, several subtracted, and different cooking techniques employed, making each dish special and different. Most homes will have a few closely guarded family secrets. Bengali cuisine is no different. For example, a dish like *ghonto* (vegetable curry) is cooked differently in different parts of Bengal. The regional variations are so vast that it will take me few more years to document these distinctions and the gastronomical delight that will follow.

Another example is of Bengal's favourite fish – *ilish* or *hilsa*. Several chapters can be written on this fish alone. Different cooking techniques along with a wide variety of ingredients to cook this fish, is mindboggling. *Ilish-er-jhol, jhal, bhape, tok, begun-diye-ilish, ilisher-paturi, ilish-sheka, ilish-pora, ilish-macher-matha-diye chocchori*, etc. The list is unending.

Bangla Gastronomy captures the essence of Bengal cuisine with its subtleties and unique influences, without going into regional differences and extreme nuances. I believe this book will ignite the desire of my readers to keep exploring this amazing cuisine from their own homes.

Why this book?

More often than not, the word Bengali evokes images of all that is succulent, syrupy, luscious, and not the Bengali beauties alone! *Bangla Gastronomy* will unleash your gastronomical desire and curiosity for all that is Bengali. Each recipe has been prepared and cooked by me personally innumerable times. It is tried, tested and tasted! And what you are seeing in print is the standardised version. Try them and I am sure the result will not disappoint you.

Read, attempt, cook and enjoy the evergreen Bengal cuisine in your very own kitchen, more so if you are a non-Bengali. And for the Bengalis, you may just rediscover your State once again!

—Ananya Banerjee

This book is dedicated to:
Roshnai - my strength, Ara - my inspiration,
& Robin - my support system.

ACKNOWLEDGEMENTS

Writing a book is never a solo endeavour. Lot of people need to add loads of value to make any effort of such magnitude successful. This book is no exception. I am truly grateful to all of those who have contributed their might, big or small, to make my dream project a reality.

For the Bengali recipes and the ones that are truly appetising and worth emulating, first of all I am indebted to my mother - the reason for my existence. I have always regarded my Mom to be the best cook in the world.

My wholehearted indebtedness goes to those who had exposed me to good food from my childhood – the typical Bengali cuisine with exquisite taste and the touch of class. My learning commenced in the early days from my grandmoms, who are unfortunately no more - *didu, didibhai* and *bulu-didu*. My evergreen aunts, *boro pishima* and *choto pishima,* whose cooking even today surpasses most skilled chefs, passed on to me brilliant secret recipes. I am sincerely grateful to my mom-in-law who taught me several nuances of Bengali cuisine.

It's difficult to name one and all who have touched me in my journey to sharpen my culinary skills. They include my elders like *mashima, kakima, mamima* and *jethima.*

Needless to mention my immense gratefulness to all my friends who keep giving their unstinted encouragement and valuable advice whenever I cook something.

Special thanks to my kids: Abhishek who coined the name of the book and Roshnai, my constant source of never-ending encouragement. The book would not see the light of the day without Robin, my husband. He mentored, guided and goaded me throughout the arduous journey.

My late father, my guardian angel, who always made me believe that 'I am good at whatever I do' - continues to motivate me in every step I take in my life.

I owe heartfelt thanks to my friend Antoine Lewis who meticulously went through the entire manuscript with me to help refine it further. Thanks to Suprita Mittar, Trishita Maitra, Smita Vyas Kumar and Pia Promina Dasgupta Barve for helping me in my research to find several gems in Bengali cookery. Special thanks to Sanchita Shinde and Ayushi Garg, two gems for helping me with all the work I do.

I am sincerely grateful to my publisher, Harsha Bhatkal for believing in me, Swapna Shinde, Armaity Motafram and Anjali Sawant for their continuous support, encouragement and hard work in creating this book.

CONTENTS

BENGALI TRADITIONAL

BENGALI

Traditional

BHATHE, BATA, BHAJA, BODA, PODA

Bengalis use unique cooking techniques to add zing to their lunch and dinner, which are not commonly found elsewhere. Among the many methods the following are special to the cuisine:

Alu-Bhathe

'Bhathe' involves boiling any vegetable or lentil, then mashing and seasoning it with mustard oil or *ghee* and spices. Traditionally whole vegetables were immersed into the rice pot to boil it while rice was being cooked. For example, the exquisite *'alu-bhathe'* (boiled mashed potatoes) mixed with *ghee* or mustard oil, seasoned with salt and green chillies, is mouth watering.

My ultimate comfort food is *'alu-bhate with ghee-bhaat'* (*ghee*-rice). In many Bengali homes *alu-bhathe* is served throughout the day - whether breakfast, lunch or dinner.

'Bata' involves grinding ingredients together. Bengalis use a flat mortar pestle to grind. Not only are condiments ground for *curries*, the *'bata'* can be a dish too. For example, *'posto-bata'* (poppy seed paste) mixed with mustard oil, green chillies and salt can form the most delicious accompaniment to hot rice.

Kochu-Bata

Among various forms of *bata*, ***'kochu-bata'*** is immensely popular. It is ground taro-root-stem, mixed with fresh coconut, mustard oil, salt and sugar and usually had with rice. The first thing that comes to mind when I think of this dish is the itching or irritation of the throat that *'kochu'* causes. As a child, I used to be mortally scared of this dish. It is popularly believed that if your throat itches after eating *'kochu-bata'*, you are quarrelsome. This made me hide the fact that my throat itched on most occasions! However over time, I started liking the brilliance of this dish.

'Bhaja' refers to anything fried. Mostly marinated with turmeric powder and salt and then deep-fried. We have *'mach bhaja'* (fried fish), *jhurijhuri alu bhaja*, (deep-fried potato straws), *potol bhaja* (pointed gourd), *kumro bhaja* (pumpkin) and the list can go on endlessly.

One of the most popular *'bhaja' is* ***'begun bhaja'*** or fried eggplant. In traditional Bengali weddings, some of the initial items to be served on a *'kola pata'* (banana leaf) are a pinch of salt, lemon and a long slice of *'begun bhaja'*.

Begun-Bhaja

When you see this deep-fried beauty on your plate it means that the *bhoj* (feast) is about to begin and the *poribeshon* (serving) will start soon.

Daaler-Boda

'Boda' is a croquette made of ground meat or vegetable bound together by spices and/or eggs served solo or in savoury gravy. One example would be *'daaler-boda'* (deep-fried lentil fritters).

Most of India consumes the *'boda'* or *'vada'* as a snack. In Bengal, it is generally taken as part of the main course. It usually accompanies the *'bhaat'* and *'daal'*. When you do not feel like having a heavy meal - just rice, lentils and *'daal-er boda'* makes for a perfect lunch.

'Poda' literally means charred. Vegetables are either wrapped in banana leaves or simply roasted over gas, wood, charcoal or coal fire.

These items are so appetising that I can have a full meal with rice and any one of the above delicacies. One such example is *'begun-poda'*, charred or roasted eggplant. This dish is the Bengali version of the popular *'baingan bharta'*.

Begun-Poda

JOLOJOG & JOLKHABAR (Small Bites)

'Jolojog' are small bites that can be had at any time, including as a snack, at breakfast or teatime. The Hindi version could be 'nashta'. 'Tiffin' is another expression especially used in the southern parts of India.

Beguni & Alur Chop (Telebhaja)

Deep-fried vegetable fritters

Do you know what a Bengali cannot survive without? 'Cha' (tea), and "Cha-er-songe Ta" (more essentially the tidbits that come with tea). Bongs have an affinity to everything deep-fried. Anything fried tastes exotic, isn't it? Most of us have a Jethu (uncle) with a noticeable potbelly, who walks to the beat of his own drum, with strict dietary restrictions. I had one too. During early evening hours, I would find him sneaking around roadside stalls outside his office munching on 'telebhaja' - the very mouth-watering (chukum-chakun) Bengali snack. It's hard to resist this extremely tasty combination – deep-fried vegetable morsels teamed perfectly with a cup of hot tea.

Beguni

Gram-flour coated eggplant fritters

Ingredients

1 medium eggplant, cut into
¼ cm thick vertical slices
½ cup gram four
1 tablespoon red chilli powder
1 teaspoon sugar
1 teaspoon turmeric powder
¼ teaspoon nigella seeds
¼ teaspoon baking soda
1 teaspoon salt
2 teaspoons hot oil
Oil to deep-fry
Chaat masala or black salt, to sprinkle

Method

- Mix gram flour, red chilli powder, sugar, turmeric powder, nigella seeds, baking soda and salt in a large mixing bowl.
- Add sufficient water and mix to a smooth batter. Add hot oil and mix well. Rest the batter for 15 minutes. Heat sufficient oil in a *kadai*.
- Dip each eggplant slice in the batter and deep-fry on medium heat till golden. Drain on absorbent paper. Sprinkle some *chaat masala* or black salt over them and serve hot.

Serves: 4-6 ***Preparation Skill Level: Easy***

Beguni

Alur Chop

Alur Chop

Fried potato cutlets

Ingredients

1 cup boiled and mashed potatoes
2 teaspoons turmeric powder
1 teaspoon cumin powder
1 teaspoon coriander powder
1 teaspoon ginger paste
¼ teaspoon green chilli paste
Salt to taste
½ cup gram flour
¼ teaspoon baking soda
2 teaspoons hot oil
Oil to deep-fry

Method

- Take mashed potatoes in a large mixing bowl.
- Add 1 teaspoon turmeric powder, cumin powder, coriander powder, ginger paste, green chilli paste and salt and mix well.
- Divide into equal portions and shape them into balls.
- Mix gram flour, remaining turmeric powder, baking soda and salt in another mixing bowl. Add sufficient water and mix into a smooth batter.
- Add hot oil and mix well. Rest the batter for 15 minutes.
- Heat sufficient oil in a *kadai*.
- Dip each potato ball in the batter and deep-fry on medium heat till golden. Drain on absorbent paper.
- Serve hot.

Serves: 3-4 ***Preparation Skill Level: Easy***

Phool Kopir Shingara

Fried stuffed dough pockets

The winter chill in Bengal can be rather biting. But for me, those were the best days. My Mom would order the tasty 'phool kopir shingara' (cauliflower samosa) for breakfast from the local 'mishtir-dokan' (sweet meat shops). On weekends, she would make it at home – hot and crispy with the tingling taste of chillies and the unmistakable winter cauliflower. While this crispy savoury treat is very Bengali, elsewhere in India, samosas are usually stuffed with potatoes and green peas. 'Shingara' when had with a cup of hot tea, is a very satisfying treat.

Ingredients

Filling

1 cup small florets of cauliflower

1 cup small cubes of potatoes

2 tablespoons green peas

1 teaspoon *panch phoron*

1 dried red chilli, broken into small pieces

A pinch of asafoetida

1 teaspoon turmeric powder

1 teaspoon red chilli powder

1 teaspoon cumin powder

1 teaspoon coriander powder

2 green chillies, finely chopped

2 tablespoons oil

1 teaspoon sugar

Salt to taste

Dough

1 cup refined flour

2 tablespoons oil

½ teaspoon salt

Oil to deep-fry

Method

- Prepare a smooth dough with flour, oil and water.
- Cover the dough with damp cloth and rest for ½ hour.
- Heat oil in a pan. Add *panch phoron,* red chilli pieces and asafoetida and sauté till light brown.
- Add potatoes and cauliflower and sauté for 2 minutes. Cover and cook till tender.

- Add turmeric powder, red chilli powder, cumin powder, coriander powder. Add chopped green chillies. Mix well and cook till the mixture becomes homogenous.
- Add sugar and salt to taste. Mix well. Keep aside to cool.
- Divide the dough into small equal portions and shape them into balls.
- Roll each of them into an oval shape. Cut each oval into 2 parts.
- Shape each part like a cone by joining two ends of the semi-circle.
- Place 2 teaspoons of filling into the hollow of each cone and seal the edges to secure the filling.
- Heat sufficient oil in a *kadai*.
- Deep-fry each *shingara* on medium heat till golden brown.
- Drain on absorbent paper.

Note: *'Mangshor shingara' (mutton keema samosa), a famous Bengali delicacy, can be prepared the same way as 'phool kopir shingara' substituting the cauliflower with mutton keema.*

Serves: 4-6 ***Preparation Skill Level: Moderate***

Ghoogni

Spicy dried peas curry

During schooling days, tiffin time meant running to the 'ghoogni-wala'. My school being of the strict disciplinarian variety, our hunger saviour was not allowed inside the campus. Through the iron gates, we would extend our arm with the exact change, only to receive one of the most delicious and tangy concoction served on 'tal-pata thonga' (palm-leaf cones). The 'ghoogni' used to be topped with tamarind water mixed with secret spices, chaat masala and a dash of lemon juice. I have tried to replicate this heavenly taste and the recipe given here is an ode to my dear old 'ghoogni-wala'.

Ingredients

1 cup dried white peas, soaked overnight and boiled

1 tablespoon mustard oil

1 teaspoon cumin seeds

A pinch of asafoetida

1 tablespoon small pieces of fresh coconut

½ cup chopped tomatoes

1 teaspoon red chilli powder

1 teaspoon turmeric powder

1 teaspoon ginger paste

1 teaspoon cumin powder

Salt to taste

1 teaspoon sugar

1 tablespoon *ghee*

1 teaspoon roasted and powdered cumin seeds

2 dried red chillies

Method

- Heat mustard oil in a pan. Add cumin seeds and asafoetida and sauté for a few seconds. Add the coconut pieces and sauté well till light brown.
- Add tomatoes, chilli powder, turmeric powder and ginger paste and sauté for 2 minutes. Add boiled peas, cumin powder, salt and sugar and cook till the mixture comes to a boil. Add water to adjust the consistency and let the mixture come to a boil again.
- Drizzle *ghee* on top. Sprinkle roasted and powdered cumin seeds and red chillies. Serve hot.

Serves: 4-6 ***Preparation Skill Level: Easy***

NANA-ROKOM BHAAT (Miscellaneous Rice-Based Preparations)

Bengalis are traditionally rice eaters. 'Bhaat' (rice) is grown abundantly in Bengal and is eaten at lunch, dinner and even breakfast. In order to make the rice-preparations interesting, numerous concoctions have been developed over the years.

Basanti Pulao

An aromatic rice preparation with a yellow hue

You can smell the Basanti pulao from a distance. The word 'Basanti' quite literally means the colour, yellow. A perfect triumvirate of flavours, this dish has a unique style of preparation. Ghee, rice and dry fruits put together in their raw form and cooked to perfection. It has a slightly sweetish taste, accented by a fruity and nutty note. I still remember how my grandmom (Bulu-didu) an acclaimed cook in the family, would make this delicious dish during special occasions, calling it 'poloa'. After multiple requests and cajoling, she agreed to teach me. I owe this recipe to her.

Ingredients

1 cup *Gobindo bhog* rice (a type of fragrant-rice) or any other aromatic rice, soaked and drained

½ cup *ghee*

Salt to taste

1 tablespoon sugar, or as per taste

1 teaspoon turmeric powder

3-4 dried red chillies, broken

2 tablespoons raisins

2 tablespoons chopped cashewnuts

1 teaspoon cumin seeds

Whole *garam masala* (2 each of green cardamoms, cloves, cinnamon sticks and bay leaves)

2 cups water

Method

- Take the rice in a bowl, add *ghee*, salt, sugar, turmeric powder, red chillies, raisins, cashewnuts and cumin seeds and mix well. Add the whole *garam masala* and bay leaves. Mix well.
- Pour 2 cups water in a deep pan, add rice mixture and mix well. Cook on medium heat for 15-18 minutes, or till the rice is fully cooked. Serve hot.

Serves: 2-3 ***Preparation Skill Level: Easy***

Khichuri

Rice and lentil porridge

It was no less than a shocker when I first got to know that 'khichuri' (khichdi) was meant for the sick in most parts of India. For Bengalis it is just as grand as it could possibly get! This dish usually has three versions. First, the delicious 'Bhog-er Khichuri' (God's prasad); second, the unforgettable combination of Khichuri with 'ilish-maach-bhaja' (fried hilsa fish) on a rainy day; and lastly as comfort food - the winning pair of khichuri with 'begoon-bhaja' (fried eggplant) savoured on a lazy Sunday. A little downpour in Kolkata, a phrase like "khichuri howe jaak aaj" (let there be 'khichuri' today) is very commonly heard.

Ingredients

1 cup *Gobindo bhog* rice

1 cup roasted split skinless green gram

2 tablespoons mustard oil

1 bay leaf

3-4 green cardamoms

1 inch cinnamon

2 teaspoons cumin seeds

1 dried red chilli

2 tablespoons scraped fresh coconut

4 green chillies, slit

1 cup diced mixed vegetables (cauliflower, beans, carrots, potatoes)

1 teaspoon turmeric powder

1 teaspoon ginger paste

1 tablespoon red chilli powder

Salt to taste

1 teaspoon sugar

2 teaspoons *ghee*

1 teaspoon *garam masala* powder

8 cups water

Method

- Soak the rice and roasted green gram separately in sufficient water.
- Heat mustard oil in a deep pan. Add bay leaf, cardamoms, cinnamon and cumin seeds and sauté till fragrant.
- Add dried red chilli, coconut and green chillies and sauté for ½ minute. Add green gram and mixed vegetables. Add turmeric powder, ginger paste and chilli powder and mix well. Add rice. Add 8 cups water and salt and cook till vegetables, rice and green grams are cooked. Add sugar and mix.
- Drizzle *ghee* and sprinkle *garam masala* powder and mix. Serve hot.

Serves: 3-4 ***Preparation Skill Level: Easy***

LUCHI/POROTA (Bengali-Style Bread)

Despite their love for rice or 'bhaat', Bengalis cannot live without 'Luchi' and 'Porota'. More importantly Bengalis love 'maida' (refined flour) unlike rest of India where 'atta' is more popular. Perhaps the Bengalis love a dose of 'fair and lovely' in their food.

Dhakai Porota

Layered and flaky fried flat bread

While some say this dish originated in Dhaka, others argue that it was a delicacy invented by the local street stalls of North Kolkata. When I was young, I remember having the famous dish from Darik's sweet-meat shop, with their special Sunday breakfast offers! Without this tasty dish, our Sunday breakfast would remain incomplete. 'Dhakai Porota' dunked in cholar daal - a combo made in heaven.

Ingredients

1 cup refined flour

Salt to taste

1 tablespoon oil + to deep-fry

½ cup milk

2 tablespoons *ghee*

2 tablespoons rice flour

Method

- Knead together refined flour, salt, 1 tablespoon oil, milk and sufficient water to a soft and pliable dough.
- Cover with a damp cloth and rest the dough for 20 minutes.
- Divide the dough into lime sized portions and shape them into balls. Roll out each ball into 8 cm circles. Apply *ghee* on the surface of each circle and sprinkle some rice flour. (This process will enable the layers to be visible once the *porota* is fried later).
- Make an incision from the centre of the circle till the edge and start rolling from one cut edge till the end to make a cone. Flatten the cone from both ends and roll it out again to a *porota* of 6 cm in diameter.
- Heat sufficient oil in a *kadai*. Deep-fry the *porotas*, one at a time, till golden and crisp. Drain on absorbent paper. *Dhakai porota* is best had with *cholar daal*.

Serves: 3-4 ***Preparation Skill Level: 3-4***

Luchi

Fried puffed bread

"Shashtir din aar maa-er onjoli" (beginning of Durga-puja and offerings to Goddess), the day when all the members of every Bengali family are fasting; breaking the fast with 'luchi' (puri) and 'aloo-chorchori' (potato sabzi) is something many would long for. I fondly remember the joint family days when an undocumented ritual ran in our family. A competition as to who would have the maximum number of luchis would take place. Choto-pishi (aunt), who was the thinnest, was always the winner, consuming over 30 luchis at a time! What a treat it is even today, when hot, freshly prepared luchis are served with an accompaniment like 'begun bhaja'.

Ingredients

1 cup refined flour

Salt to taste

1 tablespoon oil or *ghee*

Oil to deep-fry

Method

- Knead together flour, salt, oil or *ghee* and water to a smooth and pliable dough. Cover with a damp cloth and keep aside for 20 minutes.
- Heat sufficient oil in a *kadai.*
- Divide the dough into small marble sized balls. Dab each ball with a little oil and flatten slightly. Roll them out into 5 inch diameter discs.
- Heat sufficient oil in a *kadai.*
- Deep-fry the *luchis,* one at a time, in hot oil till puffed up and lightly coloured. Drain on absorbent paper.
- Serve hot with *aloo chorchori* or *begun bhaja.*

Serves: 3-4 ***Preparation Skill Level: Easy***

Radhaballabi

Spicy urad-daal stuffed fried bread

'Radhaballabi' is just a classier version of the quintessential 'hing-er kochuri', which is available usually in street corners of Kolkata. Instead of the street stalls where office goers would stop by for a cost-effective 'kochuri' meal, 'radhaballabi' is served on special occasions. When I was young, my sole attraction to attend a biye-baari (marriage ceremony) would be to have radhaballabi with aloor-dom; while others would perhaps be waiting for other delicacies.

Ingredients

1 cup refined flour

Salt to taste

1 tablespoon oil or *ghee*

Oil to deep-fry

Stuffing

1 cup white lentil *(urad dal)*

1 inch ginger

4 dried red chillies

4 cloves

4 green cardamoms

1 tablespoon fennel seeds

⅓ cup mustard oil

1 teaspoon nigella or onion seeds

A pinch of asafoetida

Salt to taste

Method

- Wash and soak the white lentil for 4-6 hours. Drain and grind with ginger, red chillies, cloves, cardamoms, fennel seeds and very little water to a smooth paste.
- Heat mustard oil in a pan, add lentil paste and sauté. Add onion seeds, asafoetida and salt and sauté till fragrant and dry. Keep aside to cool.
- Knead together flour, salt, oil or *ghee* and water to a smooth and pliable dough. Cover with a damp cloth and keep aside for 20 minutes.
- Divide the dough into equal sized balls. Take each ball in your palm and spread a little. Put some filling mixture in the centre and gather the edges and pinch them to seal. Further roll them out into slightly thick *puris*.
- Heat sufficient oil in a *kadai*. Deep-fry the *radhaballabi*, one at a time, till golden and crisp. Drain on absorbent paper. Serve hot with *aloor dom*.

Serves: 3-4 ***Preparation Skill Level: Moderate***

Koraishutir Kochuri

Green peas stuffed puri (deep-fried puffed bread)

'Koraishutir kochuri' is a delectable winter specialty! A very tasty snack, it can be had as a quick meal or when you are on the go on a busy day. While traditionally deep-fried, but if you roast them on a non-stick tawa (griddle pan), it would be so much healthier – after all we have to watch our daily calorie intake, don't we?

Ingredients

Dough

1 cup refined flour

1 tablespoon oil

Salt to taste

Ghee for cooking

Filling

1 cup fresh shelled green peas

½ inch ginger

2 green chillies

1 pinch asafoetida

1 teaspoon sugar

Salt to taste

2 tablespoons mustard oil

Method

- Knead together refined flour, oil, salt and sufficient water to a soft and pliable dough. Cover with damp cloth and keep aside.
- Grind together green peas, ginger, green chillies, asafoetida, sugar and salt to a coarse paste. Heat 2 tablespoon mustard oil in a pan. Add the paste and sauté till most of the moisture evaporates and the mixture leaves the sides of the pan. Keep aside to cool. Divide the dough into lime sized balls.
- Roll each dough ball into 3 inch diameter discs. Place 2 teaspoons filling in the centre of each disc. Bring the ends together and seal to completely cover the filling. Roll out each stuffed dough ball as thinly as possible, making sure that the filling does not ooze out. Traditionally, this rolled, stuffed dough is deep-fried in oil to prepare *kochuri*.
- Alternatively, heat a non-stick *tawa*. Place the stuffed *parathas*, one at a time and roast. Flip, drizzle a little *ghee*, flip again and drizzle some *ghee* all around. (Traditionally, *koraishutir kochuri* or *daal puri* is deep-fried. This is a healthier version as roasting them on a *tawa* minimizes the usage of fat.) Cook, turning sides till golden on both sides. Serve hot.

Serves: 3-4 ***Preparation Skill Level: Moderate***

Daal Puri

Fried puffed bread, filled with mildly spiced cholar daal (Split Bengal gram)

My grandmother was a fabulous cook. She would always cook up something special when we visited her. I vividly recall the super soft, melt in the mouth 'daal-puri' she used to make which would disappear in no time. Me and my cousins used to queue up for our turn! Alas! If only I had the ways and means to revisit my childhood! It is a great combination to have with 'alur-dom' (potato curry, Bengali-style) - a crowd puller. I hereby present to you, yet again, a healthier version of the delicacy without compromising on the taste. Instead of deep-frying, use a tawa and pan roast – after all, health is wealth.

Ingredients

Dough

1 cup refined flour

2 tablespoons oil

Salt to taste

Ghee for cooking

Filling

1 cup split Bengal gram (cholar daal), soaked

¼ teaspoon asafoetida

1 tablespoon minced ginger

2-3 garlic cloves (optional)

3-4 green chillies

1 tablespoon cumin seeds

1 tablespoon coriander seeds

2 dried red chillies

2 tablespoons oil

2 teaspoons sugar

Salt to taste

Ghee or refined oil as required

Method

- Knead together flour, oil, salt and sufficient water to a soft and pliable dough. Cover with a damp cloth and keep aside.
- Drain and cook the split Bengal gram with 2 cups water till soft.
- Cool and grind to a coarse paste with asafoetida, ginger, garlic (if using), green chillies, cumin seeds, coriander seeds and red chillies.
- Heat 2 tablespoons oil in a pan, add the paste and sauté till fragrant and dry. Add sugar and salt and mix well.

- Divide the dough into lime sized balls. Roll each dough ball into 3 inch diameter disc. Place 2 teaspoons filling in the centre of each disc. Bring the ends together and seal to completely cover the filling. Take one stuffed dough ball and roll out as thinly as possible, making sure that the filling does not ooze out.
- Heat a *tawa*. Place the stuffed *parathas*, one at a time, on it and roast. Flip, drizzle a little *ghee* all around and flip again.
- Drizzle some more *ghee* all around and cook, turning sides, till evenly golden on both sides. Serve hot.

Serves: 3-4 ***Preparation Skill Level: Moderate***

DAAL (Lentils)

Daal is the most popular accompaniment with 'Bhaat' (rice) and sometimes even 'Luchi' (fried Bengali bread); Daal is an essential part of the Bengali main course.

Tetor Daal

Moong soup with bitter gourd

Baba (my father) was always strict about taking meals in a specific sequence. I did not understand the logic, neither did I enjoy following that code of conduct until I was much older. Bengalis typically start a meal with 'teto' (bitter), which leads to the secretion of the digestive enzymes and makes it easier to binge on what comes next. This is an unusual preparation, where bitter gourd is used in the daal. It acts as a coolant for the stomach and is perfect during summers.

Ingredients

1 cup split skinless green gram (moong daal), boiled with ½ teaspoon ginger paste

1 small bitter (*teto*) gourd, cut into roundels and deep-fried

1 tablespoon mustard oil

1 teaspoon *methi* seeds

1 bay leaf

Salt to taste

1 teaspoon sugar

1 teaspoon melted *ghee*

Method

- Heat mustard oil in a *kadai*. Add methi seeds and bay leaf. Once the seeds splutter, add fried bitter gourd roundels and boiled grams and mix well.
- Bring the mixture to a boil. Add salt and sugar and mix well.
- Sprinkle *ghee* on top.

Serves: 4-6 ***Preparation Skill Level: Easy***

Cholar Daal

Sweetish Split Bengal gram soup with chopped coconut

A delicious lentil dish cooked with chana daal (split Bengal gram). It is slightly sweet, mildly spicy and is packed with nutrition. This is one of the best brunch options among several authentic Bengali recipes. 'Luchi' and 'cholar daal' is truly a match made in heaven. 'Sreehori Mishtan Bhandar', the small sweet shop in Bhawanipur in Kolkata, perhaps makes it the best. I still remember having the 'cholar daal' even without the luchi – needless to say, the taste still lingers.

Ingredients

1 cup split Bengal gram, soaked
2 tablespoons scraped fresh coconut
2 tablespoons mustard oil
A pinch of asafoetida
2 dried red chillies
1 bay leaf
1 teaspoon cumin seeds
2 green cardamoms
2 one-inch sticks of cinnamon
2 cloves
1 tablespoon chopped fresh coconut
1 teaspoon grated ginger
1 teaspoon turmeric powder
1 teaspoon cumin powder
1 teaspoon red chilli powder
2-3 slit green chillies
1 teaspoon green chilli paste
Salt to taste
1 teaspoon sugar
1 tablespoon *ghee*

Method

- Drain the grams and cook with 2 cups water and 1 tablespoon scraped coconut. Keep aside.
- Heat mustard oil in a pan. Add asafoetida, dried red chillies, bay leaf, cumin seeds, cardamoms, cinnamon and cloves. Sauté everything till aromatic.
- Add remaining scraped coconut, chopped coconut, ginger, turmeric powder, cumin powder and red chilli powder and sauté for few seconds. Add the grams, green chillies, green chilli paste, salt and sugar and bring everything to a boil.
- Drizzle *ghee* on top of the mixture and serve hot.

Serves: 4-6 ***Preparation Skill Level: Easy***

Macher-Matha Diye Muger-Daal

Lentils with fish head

As a child, going to a biye-baari (a wedding) was a completely different experience. No caterers, no buffet system. We would sit on long benches and community tables and were served food on banana leaves. The members of the host-family would normally serve the guests. 'Macher-matha diye muger-daal' was a must feature on the lunch menu on the marriage-day. While the fish preparations at dinner would be exotic and feature the more popular fish portions, the fish head was used judiciously during lunchtime for the immediate family. In a Bengali kitchen nothing gets wasted. Moreover, I remember my aunts would relish the simple 'macher-matha' (fish head) much more than the grand fish curry.

Ingredients

1 fish head cut into two, deep-fried

1 cup split skinless green gram (if available use *sona moong daal*), dry roasted and boiled

1 tablespoon mustard oil

2 bay leaves

2 one-inch cinnamon sticks

2 green cardamoms

2 cloves

1 teaspoon cumin seeds

1 teaspoon turmeric powder

1 teaspoon cumin powder

1 teaspoon red chilli powder

2 teaspoons ginger paste

2-3 green chillies, slit

Salt to taste

1 teaspoon sugar

1 tablespoon *ghee*

1 teaspoon *garam masala* powder

Method

- Heat mustard oil in a pan. Add bay-leaves, cinnamon, cardamoms and cloves and sauté. Add cumin seeds and sauté for a few seconds.
- Mix turmeric powder, cumin powder and red chilli powder in a small bowl. Add 2 tablespoons water and mix to make a paste. Add the paste to the oil and mix Add ginger paste and sauté for 2-3 minutes or till oil leaves the sides of the pan. Add boiled grams, green chillies and fried fish head.
- Cook till the mixture comes to a boil. Add salt and sugar and mix well. Sprinkle *ghee* and *garam masala* powder on top. Serve hot.

Serves: 3-4 ***Preparation Skill Level: Easy***

TORI-TORKARI (Vegetable Preparations)

Though Bengalis are known for their fish and meat preparations, there are numerous delectable and unique vegetarian preparations that form an integral part of their daily meals.

Shukto

Bitter-sweet-salty vegetable curry

One of the iconic Bengali dishes of all times. As part of 'teto' to 'mishti' sequence, 'shukto' happens to come at the very beginning. It is slightly bitter in taste in its yummiest form. Normally, Gujaratis and South Indians start with mishti (sweet), however we, the Bengalis, start with 'teto' (bitter). As far as the food history of Bengal goes, the Portuguese inhabitants taught us to use milk in savoury items. 'Shukto' is a perfect example of this practice where milk is added to finish-off the dish to bring a unique flavour. For me, the 'bodi' (lentil dumplings) in 'shukto' is the best part. My brother Bobby and me used to have a competition on who could fish out the maximum number of 'bodis' from 'shukto'. I do not recollect eating at any quintessential Bengali lunch gathering which did not begin with 'shukto'.

Ingredients

2 cups raw assorted vegetables cut into medium 1 pieces (vegetables can consist of bitter gourd, red pumpkin, raw banana, potato, broad bean, eggplant, drumstick)

3 tablespoons mustard oil

A handful of *bodis* (*vadis*)

1 tablespoon mustard seeds

2 tablespoons poppy seeds

1-2 bay leaves

1 teaspoon *panch phoron*

Salt to taste

½ cup milk

1 teaspoon sugar

1 teaspoon *ghee*

2 teaspoons dry roasted and powdered *panch phoron*

1 cup water

Method

- Heat 1 tablespoon mustard oil in a pan. Fry bodis in gentle heat till golden. Drain and keep aside.
- Grind together mustard seeds and poppy seeds to a fine paste.

- Heat the remaining mustard oil in the same pan. Add bay leaves and *panch phoron* and sauté till the spices splutter.
- Add all the vegetables and sauté well. Add bodis back in the pan. Add salt and 1 cup water. Add the mustard-poppy paste, milk and sugar and mix well.
- Cover and cook till the vegetables are tender.
- Pour *ghee* on top. Sprinkle roasted *panch phoron* powder and serve hot with steamed rice.

Note: *Panch phoron is a Bengali 5-spice mix comprising of cumin seeds, nigella seeds, fennel seeds, fenugreek seeds and mustard seeds, mixed in equal proportion.*

Serves: 3-4 ***Preparation Skill Level: Moderate***

Palong-Shaag Begun-Diye

Spinach with eggplant

'Shaag' – a concoction of greens - is the simplest form of poor man's daily need of vitamins. It is a popular saying in Bengal that if anyone can have 'shakanya' or 'shaag-rice,' and is free of debts, he would be a happy person. There are endless varieties of 'shaag' in India, and Bengal is no exception. I was not particularly fond of 'shaag' during my childhood days, and my Mom would cajole me to have it by saying that it would make my hair grow like Rapunzel's. The dream of having long hair made me have my serving of 'shaag' without a murmur. Today, though my strands do not look or compare with Rapunzel's strands, but I enjoy my dose of 'palong' (spinach) over a lot of other veggies.

Ingredients

2 cups spinach (*palong saag*), washed and chopped fine

1 medium eggplant, cut into small cubes

Salt to taste

¼ teaspoon turmeric powder

3 tablespoons mustard oil

1 teaspoon nigella seeds

1 red chilli, whole

2-3 green chillies, slit

Sugar to taste

Method

- Apply salt and turmeric to eggplant cubes.
- Heat 2½ tablespoon oil in a pan. Add eggplant cubes and sauté till eggplants are cooked and slightly browned. Drain and keep aside.
- Heat remaining oil in the same pan. Add nigella seeds and red chilli and sauté for ½ minute. Add spinach and sauté till the spinach wilts.
- Add green chillies and salt and mix well. Cover and cook till all the moisture dries up and spinach is fully cooked.
- Sprinkle a little sugar and add the eggplants to the pan. Mix well till everything is well mixed.
- Serve hot.

Serves: 3-4 ***Preparation Skill Level: Easy***

Aloo Posto

Poppy seed paste with potatoes

I feel most Bengalis go weak in their knees when they hear the term 'posto'. It's widely grown in places like Bankura and Birbhum. Many Bengali families, especially the ones in rural Bengal have 'posto' on a regular basis. 'Posto' is a sleep inducer. There is nothing like taking an afternoon nap after a 'posto-bhaat' lunch – and I would miss anything for my "posto-sleep".

Ingredients

5-6 medium potatoes, cut into small cubes and soaked in water

4 tablespoons poppy seeds

3 tablespoons mustard oil

½ teaspoon nigella seeds

Salt to taste

½ teaspoon sugar

2 green chillies, slit

Method

- Soak poppy seeds in 1 cup warm water for 15-20 minutes. Drain and grind to a fine paste.
- Heat 2 tablespoons mustard oil in a pan; add nigella seeds and sauté briefly.
- Add potato pieces and sauté on medium heat for 5 minutes, stirring frequently.
- Add poppy seeds paste mixed in ½ cup water and mix well. Cover and cook on low heat till the potatoes are done.
- Add salt, sugar and green chillies and mix well. Sauté on high heat and sprinkle 1 tablespoon raw mustard oil. Serve hot.

Chef's Tips

You can also prepare this recipe with jhinge (ridge gourd), with or without aloo (potato), potol (pointed gourd), phoolkopi, (cauliflower) or chingri (prawns).

Serves: 4-6 ***Preparation Skill Level: Easy***

Mochar Ghonto

Dry spiced banana-blossoms preparation

It is a beautiful symphony of many ingredients put together. Every year during "Narayan Pujo", we would be on a strict vegetarian diet for one whole month. The delicious 'mochar ghonto' was one of the dishes offered to God, during this time. Oh! I remember the exquisite taste of my grandma's preparation. The dish accounts for a lot of hard-work and it is a tiresome process to achieve perfection in this dish. Cutting 'mocha' has always been one of my greatest fears. I feel the generations to come after us will perhaps never know about this dish. Here is my attempt to keep the tradition alive.

Ingredients

1 banana blossom (*mocha*) finely chopped, boiled and mashed

3 tablespoons mustard oil

2-3 bay leaves

1 teaspoon cumin seeds

2 medium potatoes, boiled, peeled and cut into cubes

1 teaspoon red chilli powder

1 teaspoon cumin powder

1 teaspoon turmeric powder

1 tablespoon raisins

Salt to taste

1 teaspoon sugar

1 teaspoon *ghee*

¼ teaspoon *garam masala* powder

2 tablespoons scraped fresh coconut

Method

- Heat mustard oil in a pan, add bay leaves and cumin seeds and sauté till fragrant. Add potatoes and sauté till light brown.
- Add boiled banana blossom and sauté well. Add chilli powder, cumin powder and turmeric powder and mix well.
- Add raisins, salt and sugar. Mix well and cook for few minutes till everything is combined well. Add *ghee*, sprinkle *garam masala* powder and scraped coconut and mix lightly. Served best with plain white rice.

Chef's Tips

Bengalis make this dish with prawns also, which will then be termed as 'mocha-chingri'.

Serves: 3-4 **Preparation Skill Level: Difficult**

Ecchor-Er Dalna

Raw jackfruit curry

Ecchor is also known as 'gaachh patha' (tree goat). In very local terms, it is often referred to as, vegetarian 'mangsho' (meat). That's right. Jackfruit, if prepared well, tastes just like mutton. For those who cannot tolerate the smell of meat, this is a pretty good substitute. My first experience with this dish was at school, from my friend's tiffin box. The next time I met her mother I complimented her on her great expertise in making mutton curry. Of course it was only 'ecchor-er kosha'. (Here in this book, I am sharing a simple 'dalna' recipe.) For 'echor–kosha', please see the recipe for 'kosha mangsho' and substitute the mutton with 'ecchor' – and I assure you that you will love the vegetarian version of the dish.

Ingredients

1 medium raw jackfruit, cut into cubes and boiled

2 tablespoons mustard oil

1 teaspoon cumin seeds

1-2 bay leaves

2 medium potatoes, cut into cubes

1 medium tomato, finely chopped

1 teaspoon ginger paste

1 teaspoon turmeric powder

1 teaspoon red chilli powder

1 teaspoon cumin powder

Salt to taste

Sugar to taste

1 teaspoon *ghee*

¼ teaspoon *garam masala* powder

1 cup water

Method

- Heat mustard oil in a pan. Add cumin seeds and bay leaves and sauté till fragrant. Add potatoes and sauté till light brown.
- Add tomato, ginger paste, turmeric powder, chilli powder and cumin powder and mix well. Sauté till oil separates from the *masala*.
- Add salt and sugar to taste and mix well. Add boiled jackfruit and mix well.
- Add 1 cup water and bring to a boil. Cook till desired consistency is reached.
- Drizzle *ghee* and sprinkle *garam masala* powder on top.
- Served best with porota *(parathas), chapatti* or rice.

Serves: 4-6 ***Preparation Skill Level: Moderate***

Dhokar Dalna

Curry made of fried lentil cakes

I have always wondered how a dish so delicious can be synonymous with the word 'betrayal' ('Dhoka' means betrayal in many Indian languages). However, "ei dhoka ta khub bhalo dhoka!" - a betrayal worth enjoying!

Ingredients

1 cup split Bengal gram, soaked

1 cup split yellow peas *(matar daal)*

4-5 green chillies

Salt to taste

2 teaspoons sugar

A pinch of asafoetida

4 tablespoons mustard oil + to shallow-fry

1-2 bay leaves

1 teaspoon cumin seeds

1 teaspoon ginger paste

1 teaspoon turmeric powder

1 teaspoon red chilli powder

1 teaspoon cumin powder

1 teaspoon *ghee*

¼ teaspoon *garam masala* powder

Handful of fresh coriander leaves to garnish

Method

- Soak both Bengal gram and split yellow peas for 6-8 hours. Drain and grind them to a paste with 2-3 green chillies, salt, 1 teaspoon sugar and asafoetida.
- Heat 2 tablespoons mustard oil in a non-stick pan. Add the ground paste and sauté till the moisture dries up and the paste leaves the sides of the pan.
- Transfer the mixture onto an oiled plate and spread it evenly. Cut into diamond shaped pieces.
- Heat sufficient mustard oil in a pan and shallow-fry these diamonds till golden. Drain on absorbent paper and keep aside.
- For making the gravy, heat remaining mustard oil in the same pan. Add bay leaves and cumin seeds and cook till the seeds change colour. Mix ginger paste, turmeric powder, chilli powder and cumin powder with little water to make a paste.
- Add the paste to the oil and sauté till oil separates from the *masala*. Add 2 -3 cups water and mix well and bring the gravy to a boil.

- Add the fried lentil-diamonds to the gravy and mix gently. Let the gravy simmer till it thickens a bit. Sprinkle *ghee* and *garam masala* powder on top.
- Garnish with coriander leaves and serve hot.

Chef's Tips

- *The bodas or the diamond-shaped lentil cakes absorb moisture very fast. So even if the gravy appears to be a little watery, I would advise you to let it be because the 'bodas' will eventually soak most of the gravy.*
- *To make a non-vegetarian variation, you may add prawn paste to the lentils while grinding.*
- *The lentil cakes by themselves make a perfect party or cocktail snack.*

Serves: 4-6 ***Preparation Skill Level: Moderate***

Aloor Dom

Spiced potato curry

'Aloor Dom' is a pan-Indian dish since it can be made in many ways and consumed. Most states of India have their own version of this dish. Bengalis usually have it with luchi, bhaat, porota or ruti. 'Bijoya Dashami' (Dassehra) is an occasion to wish, hug (kolakuli) and gorge on food. Every year on this day, whenever we would visit my Jethima (aunt) to take her blessings, she would treat us with her version of this dish made without onion and garlic. It was remarkable how she managed to make it so very tasty without using the very basic ingredients. I have shared a regular 'aloor-dom' recipe and not the 'niramish' (without onion-garlic) version made at some homes.

Ingredients

2 cups boiled and peeled baby potatoes

4 tablespoons mustard oil

1 teaspoon cumin seeds

1 teaspoon turmeric powder

Salt to taste

1 teaspoon red chilli powder

1 teaspoon cumin powder

1 teaspoon coriander powder

1 teaspoon sugar

1 tablespoon *ghee*

½ teaspoon *garam masala* powder

1 teaspoon roasted cumin-red chilli powder

½ cup water

Grind together

1 medium onion

2 medium tomatoes

½ inch ginger

1 green chilli

Method

- Heat 2 tablespoons mustard oil in a pan.
- Add cumin seeds and cook till they turn a light brown. Add potatoes and sauté well.
- Add ½ teaspoon turmeric powder and salt and cook till the potatoes get a light brown colour. Drain into a bowl and keep aside.
- Heat remaining oil in the same pan. Add the ground paste and sauté for 2-3 minutes.

- Add chilli powder, remaining turmeric powder, cumin powder and coriander powder and mix.
- Add salt and sugar and mix well. Sauté till the *masala* leaves the sides of the pan. Add the sautéed potatoes and mix. Add ½ cup water and bring it to a boil and cook till the gravy thickens a bit.
- Add *ghee*, *garam masala* powder and roasted cumin-chilli powder and mix lightly.
- Served best with *luchi* or *puri* (deep-fried puffed bread).

Serves: 4-6 ***Preparation Skill Level: Easy***

Labra

Mixed vegetable preparation

'Labra', the name may seem a bit strange but actually is a medley of several vegetables. It is also known as 'chorchori' or 'panchmishali' (mixed vegetable preparation). It is not only prepared at home as part of a daily meal, but can also be enjoyed at special occasions like biye-baari (marriage celebration). 'Labra' is also served with 'bhoger-khichuri' (offerings to the God) and usually becomes the main attraction during such bhog serving. When labra is prepared with 'macher-matha' (fish-head), it is called 'chanchra' which means 'a cunning, deceitful character'. Why a vegetable preparation so tasty, gets such a name, I am yet to figure out!

Ingredients

1 cup potato cubes

1 cup pumpkin cubes

1 cup eggplant cubes

1 cup cauliflower florets

1 cup shredded cabbage leaves

1 cup ridge gourd *(jhinge)* cubes

1 cup radish cubes

½ cup mustard oil

1 teaspoon *panch phoron* (mixture of fenugreek seeds, cumin seeds, mustard seeds, nigella seeds, fennel seeds)

2 dried red chillies

3 tablespoons scraped fresh coconut

3-4 green chillies

Salt to taste

Sugar to taste

A handful of fresh coriander leaves

Method

- Heat oil in a pan, add *panch phoron* and red chillies. When the seeds splutter, add scraped coconut and sauté for a minute. Add potatoes, pumpkin, eggplant, cauliflower, cabbage, ridge gourd and radish and sauté well. Add green chillies and salt and mix well.
- Cover and cook till all the vegetables are tender. Add sugar and mix well. Garnish with coriander leaves and serve hot.

Serves: 4-6 ***Preparation Skill Level: Easy***

Muri Ghonto

Spicy fish-head preparation

Nothing goes to waste in a Bengali kitchen. Very few cuisines uses the head of a fish. The French sometimes use it in a broth. However, Bengalis use it in its full form and totality. This is a dry rice dish with pre-fried fish head, where both are cooked together. Bhaat (rice) is so dear to Bengalis that despite this preparation having bhaat in it already, they would have it with more bhaat!

Ingredients

1 fish head, broken into pieces

½ cup *Gobindo bhog* rice (use any short grained aromatic rice if *Gobindo bhog* is unavailable)

2 tablespoons mustard oil + to shallow-fry

1-2 bay leaves

1 teaspoon cumin seeds

2 green cardamoms

2 one-inch cinnamon sticks

2 cloves

1 cup chopped onions

1 teaspoon ginger paste

1 teaspoon garlic paste

1 tablespoon tomato purée

1 teaspoon cumin powder

1 teaspoon turmeric powder

1 teaspoon red chilli powder

2 teaspoons sugar

Salt to taste

2 green chillies, slit

1 tablespoon *ghee*

1 teaspoon *garam masala* powder

Method

- Apply salt and turmeric powder to the fish head. Heat sufficient mustard oil in a pan. Add fish head pieces and shallow-fry till golden brown. Drain on a plate and keep aside.
- Heat 2 tablespoons mustard oil in another pan. Add bay leaves and cumin seeds and sauté till fragrant. Add cardamoms, cinnamon and cloves and sauté till fragrant.
- Add onions and sauté till they turn pink. Add ginger paste, garlic paste and tomato purée and sauté well.

- Add cumin powder, turmeric powder and chilli powder and sauté till all the ingredients mix well. Add sugar and salt and mix well.
- Add rice and mix well. Add green chillies and fried fish heads and cook till everything is mixed well. Add 1 cup water and cook on low heat till rice is cooked and all the water is absorbed.
- Drizzle *ghee* and sprinkle *garam masala* powder on top. Serve hot.

Serves: 3-4 ***Preparation Skill Level: Easy***

Chingri-Mach Diye Thor Chechki

Prawns with banana-stem

Every part of a banana tree has its own utility, and nothing is thrown away. The kola (banana) is the basic fruit; 'kaacha-kola' (raw banana) is made into curry; the leaves (kola pata) are used as food plates or as a wrap in a paturi (steamed dish); while the 'thor' and 'mocha' (stem and blossom) are cooked to convert into signature Bengali delicacies. It is a tedious process to remove the threads while cooking 'thor'. The recipe despite being delicious is almost lost among today's generation.

Ingredients

1 cup small prawns, cleaned and deveined

1 (14 inches) banana stem (*thor*) chopped and soaked in water

Salt to taste

1 teaspoon turmeric powder

3 tablespoons mustard oil

1 teaspoon nigella seeds

1 bay leaf

1 dried red chilli

1 teaspoons ginger paste

½ teaspoon green chilli paste

½ teaspoon cumin powder

½ teaspoon coriander powder

Sugar to taste

Method

- Boil banana stem with a little salt and ½ teaspoon turmeric powder. Drain and reserve ½ cup of the stock.
- Apply ½ teaspoon turmeric and salt to prawns.
- Heat 1 tablespoon oil in a pan. Sauté prawns for 2-3 minutes. Drain and keep aside.
- Heat 2 tablespoons oil in the same pan, add nigella seeds and sauté till fragrant. Add bay leaf and red chilli and sauté for half a minute.
- Mix ginger paste, chilli paste, cumin powder, coriander powder, remaining turmeric powder, little salt and sugar with 2-3 tablespoons of water in a small bowl.

- Add this spice-mix to the pan. Sauté and cook over medium heat until oil starts separating. Add the boiled banana stem pieces and ½ cup of reserved stock. Cook for 2-3 minutes over high heat.
- Simmer, covered, until done. Add prawns and mix well. Serve it hot with steaming hot rice.

Chef's Tips

You can try the same recipe replacing prawns with boiled split Bengal gram.

Serves: 3-4 ***Preparation Skill Level: Moderate***

Lau Chingri

Bottle gourd cooked with prawns

It was an impossible task to convince me to eat 'lau-er torkari' (bottle gourd curry). However, add 'chingri' (prawns) to it, and the dull 'lau' would be transformed! I was introduced to this dish solely due to my mother's determination to make me eat 'lau'. This dish is one of the hot favorites of Bengal. It is an unusual combination of sweet bottle gourd and shrimps.

Ingredients

1 cup peeled bottle gourd cubes, boiled

½ cup small prawns, peeled and deveined

2 tablespoons mustard oil

Salt to taste

1 teaspoon turmeric powder

1 teaspoon cumin seeds

2 green chillies

½ teaspoon cumin powder

1 teaspoon sugar

1 tablespoon chopped fresh coriander leaves

Method

- Heat 1 tablespoon mustard oil in a pan. Apply salt and ½ teaspoon turmeric powder to the prawns. Add these prawns to the pan and sauté till prawns are pink. Drain and keep aside.
- Add 1 tablespoon oil to the same pan and heat. Add cumin seeds, green chillies and cook for ½ minute. Add boiled bottle gourd and sauté well.
- Add ½ teaspoon turmeric powder, cumin powder, sugar and salt and cook for 2-3 minutes. Add the fried prawns, mix well and cook till prawns are fully done.
- Garnish with coriander leaves and serve hot.

Chef's Tips

To make the dish vegetarian, you can substitute prawns with peas and grated coconut.

Serves: 2-3 ***Preparation Skill Level: Easy***

MAACH (Fish)

It is known world over that Bengalis love their fish. 'Maach-Bhaat' (fish and rice) can put Bongs at ease almost instantly and is a staple in most homes. Bengal is endowed with plenty of sweet water fish and the community boasts of various unique techniques to prepare them.

Bhetki Macher Paturi

Mustard marinated bhetki fish enveloped in banana leaves and pan-fried

I once met a foreigner at a wedding who could not stop complaining about this dish and how over-rated he thought it was. On talking to him more about his disappointment, I found out that he ate the entire paturi with the leaf all at once, without separating the 'kola-pata' from the fish. However, he did change his opinion once I taught him the right way to have it. One more fan added to the 'paturi lover's club'!

Ingredients

1 large fillet of *bhetki* or any boneless, firm fleshed fish, cut into 2 pieces

½ teaspoon turmeric powder

2 tablespoons yellow mustard seeds

2 tablespoons black mustard seeds

4-5 green chillies

1 tablespoon dried melon seeds

Salt to taste

2 tablespoons mustard oil

2 tablespoons grated coconut

Banana leaf, cut into 2 large rectangular pieces

Method

- Soak both the mustard seeds, 2 green chillies, poppy seeds, melon seeds and salt in ½ cup water for 30 minutes. Grind to a very fine paste and transfer into a bowl.
- Place a banana leaf on the work surface. Smear a little mustard oil on the surface.
- Add turmeric powder, salt, grated coconut and remaining mustard oil to the ground paste and mix well. Apply this mixture on the fish fillets.
- Place one fish fillet on each of the oil smeared banana leaves. Place one green chilli or more on each fish piece. Close from all ends to form a parcel. Secure with toothpicks or by tying with thread.
- Place in a steamer and steam for 10-12 minutes or pan fry the parcels till the leaf is charred and the fish is cooked well. Open the parcel and enjoy with steamed rice.

Chef's Tips

- *To make it vegetarian, you can substitute fish fillet with paneer or chunks of pumpkin or broad beans or mocha (banana blossoms).*
- *Microwave the banana leaves or hold each leaf onto an open flame. This process enables the leaves to be pliable and easier to work.*

Serves: 2 **Preparation Skill Level: Easy**

Ilish Bhape

Steamed hilsa-fish curry

Ilish (hilsa) maach (fish) is closest to a Bengali's heart. For them, 'ilish' is not just a fish, it is an emotion, a feeling and a memory that makes them feel at home. This community's innate love for food and particularly fish is such that even the 'kaanta' (fish bones) does not matter. Others say that Bongs have 'radar' in their mouth by virtue of which, the fish bones gets detected and rejected. Some even claim to munch the 'kaantas' too. Not being able to enjoy 'ilish' efficiently is embarrassing for any Bengali.

Ingredients

2-3 pieces *hilsa* (*ilish*) fish

1 tablespoon black mustard seeds

1 tablespoon yellow mustard seeds

3-4 whole green chillies

Salt to taste

1 teaspoon turmeric powder

1 tablespoon yogurt

4 tablespoons mustard oil

Method

- Grind both the mustard (black and yellow) seeds with 2 green chillies and salt to a fine paste.
- Take a microwavable dish. Place hilsa fish in it. Apply salt, turmeric powder, mustard paste, yogurt and mustard oil well on the fish. Place the remaining green chillies over them.
- Cover the dish with a cling film, place it in the microwave and cook on HIGH for 3 minutes. Serve hot.

Note: *Traditionally, the marinated fish is placed in an air tight container, and steamed. Hence the name is "bhape" (steamed). But the recipe uses microwave, which helps to cook the fish faster yet the result is the same.*

Serves: 2-3 ***Preparation Skill Level: Easy***

Chingri Malai Curry

Jumbo prawns in coconut gravy

This is one of the most quintessential dishes of Bengal, and forms part of any celebratory menu. Often regarded as a Jamai (son-in-law) ador (affection) dish and is cooked on Jamai Shashti (son-in-law's day). Some say that this dish has come from Malaysia, hence the word malai or Malaya. Another opinion is that the use of coconut milk makes it creamy or 'malai-like'. Whatever be the source, this dish is delectable.

Ingredients

2-4 *golda chingri* (large lobsters or jumbo prawns), cleaned with heads intact

2 teaspoons turmeric powder

Salt to taste

5-6 tablespoons mustard oil

2 green cardamoms

1 inch cinnamon stick

2 cloves

1 teaspoon cumin seeds

1 teaspoon red chilli powder

1 teaspoon cumin powder

Sugar to taste

2 whole green chillies

Few pieces of cashewnuts

Few raisins

1 cup coconut milk

1 tablespoon *ghee*

1 teaspoon *garam masala* powder

Grind

1 large onion

1 inch ginger

1 medium tomato

Method

- Marinate the lobsters/prawns with 1 teaspoon turmeric powder and salt.
- Heat 2 tablespoons mustard oil in a pan. Add marinated lobsters/prawns and sauté till they turn orange. Drain and keep aside.
- Heat the remaining oil in the same pan. Add cardamoms, cinnamon, cloves and cumin seeds and sauté till fragrant. Add the ground paste, remaining turmeric powder, chilli powder and cumin powder and sauté till oil separates. Add sugar and salt and mix.

- Put the lobsters back in the pan. Add green chillies, cashewnuts and raisins, reserving a few for garnish. Add a little water and simmer for 2-3 minutes.
- Add coconut milk, *ghee* and *garam masala* powder and simmer for a minute.
- Serve garnished with reserved cashewnuts and raisins.

Note: *This dish can also be made with paneer.*

Serves: 2-4 ***Preparation Skill Level: Easy***

Daab Chingri

Prawns in a creamy sauce cooked in a tender coconut shell

The presentation of this dish has always intrigued me. It looks nothing like any other Bengali dish. The surprise element is when the whole coconut shell comes to the table. The secret gets revealed when one digs into the succulent pieces of prawn inside the daab (coconut). I have heard stories from my mom that long ago, when cooking was done in clay ovens, my grand mom would prepare 'daab-chingri' by putting all the ingredients inside the coconut shell and place it below the clay oven, after all the cooking was over. The residual heat from the clay oven would cook the dish to perfection. My recipe here is a tweaked version of the traditional one.

Ingredients

250-300 grams medium sized prawns, peeled and deveined

2 tablespoons mustard oil

1 tablespoon butter

½ cup chopped onions

½ teaspoon ginger paste

¼ teaspoon garlic paste

½ teaspoon green chilli paste

2 tablespoons fresh cream

½ cup tender coconut flesh, puréed (keep the tender coconut shell intact and keep some of the coconut water aside)

Salt to taste

1 tablespoon readymade mustard paste *(kashundi)* or ground mustard paste

¼ cup coconut water

1 sweet lime sized ball of wheat flour dough

Method

- Heat mustard oil in a pan, add prawns and sauté till the prawns are light pink. Drain and keep aside. Take care not to overcook.
- In the same pan, heat butter and add onions and sauté until they turn light golden. Add ginger paste, garlic paste and green chilli paste and mix well. Add fresh cream and cook for 2 minutes.
- Transfer this onion mixture, sautéed prawns and puréed tender coconut flesh into the coconut shell. Add salt, *kashundi,* ¼ cup coconut water and mix everything well. Seal the mouth of the coconut with the wheat flour dough.
- The *daab chingri* can be microwaved for 10 minutes on high or baked in a preheated oven at 250° C for 20-25 minutes. Serve hot.

Serves: 3-4 ***Preparation Skill Level: Moderate***

Rui Macher Jhol

Everyday rohu-fish watery curry

Rui maach (rohu) is usually a staple in a Bengali household. 'Maach-er jhol aar bhaat', is perfectly paired and loved by all. Growing up in Kolkata, I realised that Bongs can relish 'maach-bhaat' (fish and rice) as many times as it is offered to them in a day! During my school days, many of my friends would have 'maach-bhaat' even for breakfast, and would wind up their day with the same for dinner. Cooking for our friend Partho even today is a challenge for his wife Panchali, as she would need to get for her hubby his daily dose of 'jhol bhaat' wherever he is in the world – so addictive is 'macher-jhol' to a Bengali.

Ingredients

2 big darnes or pieces of *rohu* fish

Salt to taste

1 teaspoon turmeric powder

3 tablespoons mustard oil

1 teaspoon nigella seeds

1 medium potato, boiled, peeled and cut into long slices

1 teaspoon red chilli powder

1 teaspoon cumin powder

1 teaspoon coriander powder

2 green chillies, slit

Chopped fresh coriander leaves to garnish

2 cups water

Method

- Apply salt and ½ teaspoon turmeric powder to the *rohu* fish darnes.
- Heat 1 tablespoon mustard oil in a pan. Add the fish and shallow-fry, turning sides, till lightly coloured. Drain on a plate and keep aside.
- Add 1 tablespoon oil to the same pan. Add nigella seeds and sauté ½ a minute and add the potato. Add red chilli powder, ½ teaspoon turmeric powder, cumin powder, coriander powder, green chillies and salt.
- Sauté well and add 2 cups water and mix well to make a watery gravy. Bring the gravy to a boil and cook till the potatoes are tender. Add the fried fish and bring it to boil and cook for 2 minutes covered.
- Drizzle remaining mustard oil on top, sprinkle coriander leaves and serve hot.

Chef's Tips

Vegetables like pointed gourd, pumpkin or eggplant can be added with potatoes as variations.

Serves: 2 ***Preparation Skill Level: Easy***

Shorshe Pabda

Pabda-fish cooked in mustard gravy

'Pabda' is one of the tastiest sweet water fish. I always prefer to prepare 'pabda' for my non-Bengali friends as absence of too many bones or kaanta makes it a hit. Children as well as the lazy ones who want to enjoy the great taste without putting in the effort to extract the fish-bones equally adore it. Whenever I made 'sorshe-bata' (mustard paste), my mother-in-law would say my 'shorshe-bata' comes out the best. I did not understand the significance. She believed that when people with much anger in them prepared the mustard paste it would turn out extremely pungent (shorsher-jhaj). It is believed, people who have bitter thoughts, their mustard paste will be bitter. Therefore, when mom-in-law said my 'shorshe-bata' works, it meant a lot more than its literal meaning. It was her way of accepting the young bride into the family. Naturally I was elated!

Ingredients

4 *pabda* (a type of sweet-water fish)

1 teaspoon turmeric powder

Salt to taste

3 tablespoons mustard oil

1 teaspoon nigella seeds

2 tablespoons mustard paste (made with 2 teaspoons black mustard seeds, 2 teaspoons yellow mustard seeds, 2 green chillies and salt)

2 green chillies

2 tablespoons chopped fresh coriander leaves

Method

- Apply ½ teaspoon turmeric powder and salt to the *pabda* fish.
- Heat 2 tablespoon oil in a pan, add the fish and shallow-fry, turning sides, till both sides are evenly coloured. Drain and keep aside.
- Add 1 tablespoon oil to the oil remaining in the pan and heat. Add nigella seeds and sauté till fragrant.
- Add the mustard paste and ½ teaspoon turmeric powder. Sauté till all the moisture dries.
- Add ½ cup water, salt and green chillies and bring the gravy to a boil. Add the fried fish and cook till the gravy reduces to the desired consistency.
- Drizzle remaining mustard oil and garnish with coriander leaves. Serve hot.

Note: *Combination of half yellow mustard seeds and half black mustard seeds reduces the pungency. If you are not used to mustard, this will work better. If you are a mustard addict, you can use only the black seeds for that unmistakable mustard kick.*

Chef's Tips

Various other types of fish, like rohu, katla, bhetki or eggs or chicken can be used to make this delicious dish by following the same recipe.

Serves: 2 **Preparation Skill Level: Easy**

Doi Maach

Fish cooked with mild yogurt sauce

This is a delicate sweet and sour curry. It is quite different from the normal macher-jhol, which is usually consumed almost everyday in Bengali homes. 'Paka-dekha' is a Bengali practice wherein the alliance of the marriage is finalised. This dish featured on my engagement day. Doi (yogurt) is considered a good omen, and hence 'doi maach' is a special dish.

Ingredients

4 pieces of fish (*rui, katla or bhetki*)

4 medium onions, grate and extract the juice

Grind 2-3 inch ginger and extract about 4 tablespoons of juice

400 grams yogurt

½ tablespoon gram flour

4 tablespoons mustard oil

Salt to taste

1 tablespoon *ghee*

2 bay leaves

2 cloves

2 green cardamoms

2 one-inch cinnamon sticks

Sugar to taste

2-3 green chillies, slit

Method

- Mix onion juice, ginger juice, yogurt and gram flour well to make a smooth mixture with no lumps. Keep aside.
- Heat 2 tablespoons mustard oil in a pan. Rub salt on the fish pieces.
- Add to the pan and shallow-fry, turning sides, till both sides are evenly done. Drain on a plate and keep aside.
- Add the remaining oil to the pan along with *ghee*.
- Add bay leaves, cloves, green cardamoms and cinnamon and sauté till fragrant.

- Add the yogurt mixture and mix. Add salt and sugar and mix well.
- Let the gravy simmer on low to medium heat for a few minutes. Add fish pieces.
- Cover and cook for 2 minutes and then uncover and let the gravy thicken slightly or till the oil begins to separate.
- Garnish with slit green chillies and serve hot.

Note: *This dish can also be made with chicken or mutton or paneer as vegetarian option.*

Serves: 2-4 ***Preparation Skill Level: Easy***

Macher Ganga-Jamuna or Horogouri

Fish cooked spicy on one side and tangy on the other

Popularly known as 'macher horogouri' that stands for Shiva and Parvati. This dish is usually cooked with 'koi-maach' (climbing perch). 'Koi' being very seasonal, the dish can be made with 'tilapia' as a substitute. I learnt this recipe from Bulu-didu (my grandma). The specialty of this dish is one side is 'tok' (sour) and the other side is 'jhaal' (hot and pungent). The popular Bengali phrase: "bhaaja maach-ta ulte khete jaane na" (meaning, one is so naive, that after finishing one side of the fish, one does not know you can turn the fish over and have the other side) won't work here. This is because if you do not know how to flip, you will miss out on the yummy-taste that awaits you on the other side of the fish!

Ingredients

For Ganga

4 medium sized whole fish (preferably *koi maach* or climbing perch)

Salt to taste

1 teaspoon turmeric powder

Oil to deep-fry

2 tablespoons mustard oil

1 teaspoon nigella seeds

2 tablespoons black mustard paste

1 teaspoon red chilli powder

4-5 green chillies, slit

For Jamuna

2 tablespoons mustard oil

1 teaspoon black mustard seeds

2 teaspoons concentrated tamarind extract (diluted in 2 tablespoon of water)

½ teaspoon red chilli powder

2-3 green chillies, slit

Salt to taste

2 teaspoons sugar

Method

- Ganga preparation: Apply salt and 1 teaspoon turmeric powder on the fish. Heat sufficient oil in a pan and fry fish till brown. Drain on absorbent paper and keep aside.
- Heat 2 tablespoons mustard oil in a pan, add nigella seeds and let them splutter. Add mustard paste, red chilli powder, ½ teaspoon turmeric powder, salt and green chillies and mix. Add a little water and mix. Sauté the mixture till oil begins to separate.

- Add about ⅓ cup water and bring the gravy to a boil. Arrange the fish pieces in the gravy. Do not turn and cook till the gravy dries up a bit and the fish has this mustard gravy on one side. Keep aside.
- Jamuna preparation: Heat 2 tablespoons mustard oil in another pan, add mustard seeds and let them sputter. Add tamarind extract, red chilli powder, green chillies, salt and sugar. Add ⅓ cup water and bring the gravy to a boil.
- When the gravy comes to a boil, carefully place the fish cooked in mustard gravy with the side untouched by the mustard sauce facing down into the tamarind gravy. Cook till the gravy dries up a bit. Serve hot.

Serves: 2-4 ***Preparation Skill Level: Moderate***

Kakrar Jhal

Spicy crab curry

'Kakra' (crab) is a delicacy that is enjoyed not only in India, but also the world over. 'Kakrar-jhal' (crab-curry), according to me, can stand out as one of the best crab dishes! My first encounter with crabs was in Mandarmani, which is a seaside village in West Bengal. Red crabs crawling around the 13 km long beach is one of the specialties of this place. The funniest thing about these sneaky creatures is how they would quickly hide under the sand the moment they heard nearing footsteps or vibrations. As for its preparation, the crabs need to arrive in your kitchen 'live' as they decompose very quickly. But killing them inside the kitchen can be gruesome - I feel as if the crabs are staring right into my eyes. To make the process easier I simply put the crabs into the freezer so that they go to sleep before preparing them.

Ingredients

8 crabs, cleaned, legs separated and slightly crushed

4 tablespoons mustard oil

Salt to taste

1 teaspoon turmeric powder

½ cup onion paste

2 teaspoons ginger paste

2 teaspoons garlic paste

1 teaspoon red chilli paste

½ cup chopped tomatoes

2 teaspoons cumin powder

2 teaspoons coriander powder

Mustard paste (made with 1 tablespoon black mustard seeds, 1 tablespoon yellow mustard seeds, 2 green chillies and salt)

Sugar to taste

2-3 green chillies, slit

½ cup chopped fresh coriander leaves

Method

- Heat 2 tablespoons mustard oil in a pan. Rub a little salt and ½ teaspoon turmeric powder on the crabs.
- Add them to the pan and shallow-fry, turning sides, till they turn red in colour on both sides. Drain in a bowl and keep aside.
- Heat remaining oil in the same pan, add onion paste, ginger and garlic pastes and sauté till fragrant. Add red chilli paste and tomatoes and sauté for 5 minutes. Add cumin powder, coriander powder and ½ teaspoon turmeric powder and sauté for

30 seconds. Add mustard paste and sauté till oil separates. Add salt, sugar and fried crabs and slit green chillies. Sauté stirring continuously for 2 minutes.

- Add a little water and cover and cook for 5 minutes or till the crabs are cooked and well blended with spices. Garnish with coriander leaves and serve hot.

Note: *This dish can also be made with fish or boiled eggs.*

Serves: 6-8 ***Preparation Skill Level: Moderate***

MURGI (Chicken), MANGSHO (Mutton), DEEM (Eggs)

Meat ('murgi' or chicken and 'mangsho' or mutton) is usually served after fish is served in a traditional Bengali meal. 'Murgi' and 'mangsho' preparations could be varied - from light, flavourful, watery gravies to spicy, thick, semi-dry preparations, and they are all equally delectable. 'Deem' or eggs are also part of this sequence of meals, and is not restricted to breakfast as is popular in the rest of the world.

Robibarer Mangshor Jhol

Everyday mutton curry

'Jhol' is an everyday watery thin curry or gravy. 'Mangshor' (mutton) jhol is a famous Bengali dish and popular as Sunday special. As a resident of Kolkata, every Sunday, at around 1 pm an orchestra played in my 'para' (locality). The melodious sounds were the whistles from the pressure cookers from the neighbouring households, making the Sunday special 'mangshor-jhol' resulting our hunger pangs to grow.

Ingredients

1 kg fresh mutton, cut into medium pieces on the bone

2 tablespoons mustard oil

1 teaspoon sugar

1 bay leaf

1 cup onion-tomato paste (made with 2 medium onions, 2 inch ginger, 4-5 garlic cloves, 2 medium tomatoes)

1 teaspoon turmeric powder

1 teaspoon red chilli powder

2-3 medium potatoes, halved

Salt to taste

1-2 green chillies, slit

1 teaspoon *ghee*

¼ teaspoon *garam masala* powder

Method

- Heat mustard oil in a pressure cooker. Add sugar and bay leaf and sauté for ½ minute. Add onion-tomato paste, mix and sauté well. Add turmeric powder and red chilli powder, mix and sauté till oil leaves the sides of the cooker.
- Add potatoes and mutton and mix well. Add 2-3 cups water. Please note this will be watery gravy. Add salt and mix.

- Close the lid of the cooker and cook under pressure till 5-6 whistles are given out. (Cooking time depends on the quality of the mutton).
- Open the lid of the cooker when the pressure reduces completely. Add *ghee* and *garam masala* powder and mix well. Simmer for 5 minutes. Serve hot with rice.

Note: *This dish can also be made with chicken, fish, egg, vegetables or cottage cheese.*

Serves: 4-6 ***Preparation Skill Level: Easy***

Kosha Mangsho

Slow cooked mutton

This preparation is as iconic as it could get! 'Kosha-mangsho' and 'luchi' is one of the favourite combinations, extravagantly served in Bengali 'biye-baari' (marriage functions). It is indeed a star dish in a buffet and a crowd pleaser. It follows a very tedious process of cooking while it demonstrates the labour of love! I still remember the taste of "Gol-barir kosha mangsho" at Shyambazar crossing – it is said to have a secret recipe – putting the dish on the culinary map. I have tried to replicate its awesome taste here.

Ingredients

1 kg mutton, cut into medium sized pieces on the bone

½ cup yogurt

1 teaspoon ginger paste

1 teaspoon garlic paste

3-4 medium onions (500 grams)

2 inch ginger

4-5 garlic cloves

½ cup mustard oil

1-2 bay leaves

2-3 green cardamoms

1 inch cinnamon

2-3 cloves

2 teaspoons sugar

1 teaspoon turmeric powder

1 teaspoon red chilli powder

1-2 green chillies, slit

Salt to taste

1 tablespoon *ghee*

1 teaspoon Bengali *garam masala* (grind equal portions of cinnamon, cloves and green cardamoms)

Handful of chopped fresh coriander leaves

Method

- Mix mutton with yogurt, ginger and garlic paste in a bowl. Keep it in the refrigerator to marinate for 5-6 hours. Grind together onion, ginger and garlic.
- Heat mustard oil in pressure cooker. Add bay leaves, cardamoms, cinnamon and cloves. Add sugar and sauté till it caramelises.
- Add the onion-tomato paste, turmeric powder and chilli powder and mix well. Sauté on high heat till the oil leaves the sides of the *masala*.
- Add the marinated mutton and continue to cook on high heat till all the liquid dries up.

- Add 1 cup water, green chillies and salt and mix well. Add *ghee* and *garam masala* powder and mix well.
- Close the cooker and cook under pressure till 6-7 whistles are given out or till the mutton is tender. Cook the mutton on open flame till the gravy thickens. Traditionally it is slow cooked for 3-4 hours on open flame. If you have that kind of time in hand definitely go for it as the result can be fantastically delicious.
- Garnish with chopped coriander leaves. Best served with *luchi*.

Note: *This dish can also be made with chicken or soya.*

Serves: 4-6 ***Preparation Skill Level: Moderate to Difficult***

CHUTNEY (Relish)

Once the Bengalis have savoured the main course and are ready to move on to the dessert, they enjoy a variety of palate cleansers, which are in the form of 'chutney' or relishes. This sequence of serving is a very special concept not usually found eleswhere.

Aamer Chutney

Sweet and sour relish made with raw mangoes

We look forward to our summer vacations, don't we? As a little girl I used to wait for the summers throughout the year just to taste the homemade chutney made by my Dida (granny). The tok-mishti (sweet and sour) combination of 'kaacha-aam' (raw mango) with 'panch phoron' (Bengali five-spice) and 'bhuna jeera' powder (roasted cumin powder) was no less than an addictive drug. I still recall Dida pulling my ears for stealing 'aamer-chutney' from her kitchen every now and then.

Ingredients

2 large/4 small raw mangoes

2 cups sugar

1 tablespoon mustard oil

2 dried red chillies

1 teaspoon *panch phoron* (mix equal quantities of cumin seeds, nigella seeds, fennel seeds, fenugreek seeds and mustard seeds)

½ teaspoon turmeric powder

Salt to taste

1 teaspoon roasted cumin seeds-red chilli powder (Bhaja-moshla)

Method

- Cut mangoes into small pieces. Heat mustard oil in a pan. Add red chillies and *panch phoron* and sauté till light brown.
- Add mangoes, turmeric powder and salt. Mix well. Add 1 cup water and cook on medium heat till the mangoes are soft. Add sugar and cook till the chutney is thick and lightly caramelised.
- Sprinkle roasted cumin seeds-red chilli powder, mix and keep aside to cool. Serve at room temperature.

Chef's Tips

Sugar should be added last and not at the beginning as sugar tends to delay the cooking process.

Serves: 4-6 | ***Preparation Skill Level: Easy***

Aamshotto-Khejur-Tomatoer Chutney

Dried sweet mango pulp, dates and tomato relish

When I was in school, my grandma used to keep the 'aamshotto' layers for sun drying on our terrace. To prevent birds from pecking on it, my brothers and me were assigned duties to shoo-away the birds and crows. However, the 'aamshotto' used to be so delicious, before the crows could swoop-in, we would have already had our share of this exquisite preparation.

Ingredients

½ cup dried mango pulp sheets (*aamshotto*), roughly chopped

10 to 12 seedless dates, roughly chopped

4-6 medium tomatoes, chopped

2 tablespoons vegetable oil

1 teaspoon *panch phoron* (equal quantities of mustard seeds, cumin seeds, fennel seeds, fenugreek seeds, nigella seeds)

Salt to taste

¼ teaspoon turmeric powder

1 cup sugar

½ cup raisins

2 tablespoons roasted and powdered spices (made with 1 tablespoon cumin seeds,1 tablespoon fennel seeds and 1 dried red chilli)

Method

- Heat oil in a pan. Add *panch phoron* and sauté till fragrant.
- Add tomatoes, salt and turmeric powder and mix well. Cook till tomatoes become pulpy and totally mashed for around 5 minutes.
- Add sugar and mix. Increase heat to high and cook till the mixture thickens.
- Add dates and mix well and cook. Add *aamshotto* and raisins and mix well. Cook till the mixture thickens.
- Sprinkle roasted spice powder.

Serves: 4-6 ***Preparation Skill Level: Easy***

MISHTIMUKH (Desserts)

One can safely claim that Bengal is most known for its Mishti (sweets). The 'rosogolla' (steamed sweetened cottage cheese roundels), 'sondesh' (cottage cheese sweets) and 'mishti-doi' (sweetened-yogurt) have put Bengal at the epicentre of the world's culinary map. Foreigners visiting Bengal will never depart without tasting these super iconic sweet treats. While these varieties are found commercially in sweet-meat shops, there is another array of delicious sweets which are entirely home-made and includes 'payesh', 'pithe' and 'puli'.

Nolen Gurer Payesh

Rice pudding with freshly harvested date-jaggery

'Nolen gurer payesh' is a permanent item in our family birthday menu. My mother used to say, having 'payesh' (rice pudding or kheer or payasam) on birthdays increase longevity. Whether you are 8, 18 or 80, it is a dish widely loved by everyone. The specialty here is the use of 'nolen gur' (newly harvested date palm jaggery) instead of sugar as the sweetener. When I was in school, everyone wanted to be a friend of mine specifically around my birthday just that they could enjoy this appetising preparation made by my mom.

Ingredients

3 tablespoons rice (preferably *Gobindo bhog* rice. If unavailable use any aromatic rice like *Basmati*)

1 litre full-fat cow's milk

1 cup grated freshly harvested date-jaggery (*nolen gur*)

1 tablespoon sugar candy

1 tablespoon chopped cashewnuts

2 tablespoons raisins

Method

- Wash rice and keep aside.
- Boil milk in a heavy bottomed pot, add rice and simmer for 15 minutes or till the rice is cooked and the milk is reduced to almost half.
- Add date jaggery, sugar candy, cashewnuts and raisins and bring to a boil. Simmer till the mixture thickens.
- Best served chilled.

Notes:

- *If 'nolen gur' is unavailable, sugar can be used instead of gur. But in that case it would be called 'payesh' and not 'nolen gurer payesh'.*
- *Mishri prevents the payesh (kheer) from curdling. Sometimes impurities in the gur or jaggery tends to curdle the milk.*
- *Nolen gur is available during winter months in Bengal and at specialised outlets in larger towns in India.*

Serves: 6-8 ***Preparation Skill Level: Moderate***

Baked Rosogolla

'Rosogolla' placed in sweet-thickened milk and then baked

Bengalis can be intellectual and yet argumentative. It is impossible for me to forget the endless debates my friends had with another classmate on the origin of 'rosogolla'. You may have guessed that the other girl was from Odisha. Every day, the two would come up with solid facts to back their arguments. Kept wondering, if this research had gone into their studies, these two would have definitely topped in class. Keeping the origin of 'rosogolla' aside, Bengal definitely is responsible for popularising it as one of the most iconic Indian sweets. The recipe here is a modern take on the ever-popular dessert.

Ingredients

1 litre cow's milk

Juice of 2 lemons

1 cup sugar

½ litre full cream milk

½ tin condensed milk

½ teaspoon green cardamom powder

Method

- Boil cow's milk in a deep pan, add lemon juice and stir till the milk curdles and forms *chhana*.
- Drain the *chhana* and refresh it under running water to cool it and get rid of the lemony flavour. Drain it thoroughly and transfer onto a large plate. Knead the *chhana* well into a smooth paste without any grains.
- To check if the dough is ready, take a small portion and roll into a ball. If the ball has no cracks it is ready. Divide it into 6 equal portions and roll them into smooth balls. Keep aside.
- Pour 4 cups water into a pressure cooker, add sugar and bring the mixture to a boil. Add the *chhana* balls, one by one, close the lid of the pressure cooker (without the weight), and lower the heat. Let it cook for 6-7 minutes.
- Boil full cream milk in another pan. Add condensed milk and cardamom powder and cook, stirring, till thick *rabdri* consistency is reached. Coat the *rosogollas* in the thickened milk.
- Place the soaked *rosogollas* in a baking dish. Place under a grill so that the top gets browned and charred. You can use a blow torch, instead of a grill. Serve chilled.

Chef's Tips

Instead of baking/grilling, just boiling the rosogolla in thickened rabdi makes it 'Rosogolla-r payesh' - which is another popular Bengali dessert.

Preparation Skill Level: Easy, if 'rosogolla' is bought readymade. It could be difficult if the dish is to be made from scratch.

Serves: 6-8

Langcha

Cylindrical fried dough dipped in sugar syrup

The reason for 'langcha' to stand out despite the already existing presence of somewhat similar tasting 'gulaab-jamun' is its cylindrical shape. Shaktigarh, situated in the Burdwan district of West Bengal is famous for creating this spectacular dish. Whenever I visit this town, I am naturally drawn towards the shop "Langcha Mahal" with Uttam Kumar's (most famous Bengali film actor) posters claiming that he used to savour the enticing 'langcha' there. Story of a fan-girl's life. Sigh!

Ingredients

500 grams *chhana* (cottage cheese made by curdling cow's milk, and separating the whey)

125 grams *mawa*

100 grams refined flour

¼ teaspoon baking powder

100 grams castor sugar

Few black cardamom seeds

500 grams granulated sugar

Ghee or oil to deep-fry

1 cup water

Method

- Grate *chhana* and *mawa* into a bowl. Add flour, baking powder, castor sugar and cardamom seeds and mix well. Knead the mixture into a smooth dough.
- Boil together sugar and 1 cup water to make the sugar syrup.
- Divide the dough into equal portions and shape each into a ball. Further shape them into cylinders or *langchas*.
- Heat sufficient *ghee* or oil in a deep pan. Deep-fry the *langchas* till reddish brown. Drain the *langchas* and dip them in the syrup.
- Serve warm.

Serves: 8-10 ***Preparation Skill Level: Moderate***

Malpua

Deep-fried flour-mawa discs soaked in sugar syrup

"Mashima malpua khamu" (Aunty, want to eat 'malpua'?) is one of the most famous dialogues uttered by one of the greatest Bengali comedians Bhanu Bandopadhyay, in the movie "Lukochuri". 'Malpua' almost became a household name thereafter. It is the traditional Indian version of a pancake, which is served as a dessert. In India, most regions have their own version of this appealing dish.

Ingredients

Batter

4 tablespoons milk powder

2 tablespoons mawa

3 tablespoons refined flour

5 tablespoons milk

1 tablespoon castor sugar

1 tablespoon semolina

Ghee as required

Sugar syrup

1 cup sugar

A pinch of green cardamom powder

½ cup water

Method

- Take milk powder, mawa, refined flour, milk, sugar and semolina in a bowl and whisk together to make a smooth batter. Rest it for 1 hour.
- Cook together sugar, ½ cup water and green cardamom powder till you get a thick syrup. Keep it warm.
- For each *malpua* heat 2 teaspoons *ghee* in a pan. Drop 1 ladleful of batter and shallow-fry, turning sides, till both sides are golden brown.
- Drain the *malpuas* and immerse them in the sugar syrup for a little while.
- Serve warm or cold.

Serves: 3-4 ***Preparation Skill Level: Moderate***

Lobongo Latika

Sweetened stuffed pastry secured with clove (lobongo)

I was always intrigued by the term 'lobongo latika' especially due to its unique and flowery tone. It was more fascinating when some parents named their daughters "Latika" – perhaps they did so out of sheer love for this evergreen dessert! Whenever my family would go on a picnic, they would carry this sweet due to its crispiness and its long lasting quality. It is a handy dessert to be had on the go.

Ingredients

Dough

1 cup refined flour

1 tablespoon *ghee*

2 tablespoons powdered sugar

¼ teaspoon salt

8-10 cloves

Oil to deep-fry

Sugar syrup

1 cup sugar + 1 cup water

Filling

1 tablespoon *ghee*

1 tablespoon chopped cashewnuts

2 tablespoons raisins

2 tablespoons semolina

1 tablespoon powdered sugar

1 tablespoon scraped fresh coconut

1 cup *mawa*

Method

- Mix flour, *ghee*, sugar and salt in a bowl, add sufficient water and knead into a soft dough. Cover with a damp cloth and keep aside for 15 minutes.
- For filling heat *ghee* in a pan. Add cashewnuts, raisins, semolina, sugar, coconut and *mawa* and cook till thick. Keep aside to cool. Cook together sugar and 1 cup water in another pan to make a thick syrup. Keep it warm. Divide the dough into small equal portions and shape them into balls.
- Roll the balls into ovals. Place 2 teaspoons of filling in the centre of each oval. Fold from all sides like an envelope and secure with a clove. These are *lobongo latika*.
- Heat sufficient oil in a *kadai* and deep-fry the *lobongo latika* till golden brown and crisp. Drain and dip them in the sugar syrup till they are well coated with the syrup. Serve cold.

Serves: 6-8 ***Preparation Skill Level: Moderate***

Ice-Cream Sondesh

Flavoured frozen sweet cottage cheese cubes

Sondesh is the mouthwatering dessert which every Bengali would have grown up with. Then came the British influence of serving ice-creams at parties. Innovation at its best – some sweetmeat entrepreneur simply combined the two delicacies to make one outstanding dessert – ice-cream sondesh. Try it, and you will love it.

Ingredients

2 cups *chhana* (made by curdling cow's milk. Then draining in a muslin cloth)

½ teaspoon vanilla essence

½ cup condensed milk

1 teaspoon butter

Garnishing

Few almonds, sliced

Few pistachios, sliced

Few saffron strands

Method

- Mix *chhana*, vanilla essence and condensed milk in a bowl.
- Put the mixture into a blender and blend.
- Grease a steal box with butter, transfer this mixture into the box and close the box with a tight fitting lid.
- Heat some water in a pressure cooker, place the box in it and close the cooker. Cook without the pressure for 12-15 minutes.
- Take the cooker off the heat and let it cool down to room temperature.
- Keep the box in the freezer and freeze till set.
- Cut into pieces, garnish with almonds, pistachio and saffron.
- Serve chilled.

Yield: 8-10 pieces ***Preparation Skill Level: Easy***

Mishti Doi

Sweetened yogurt

If you are at the Kolkata airport, you are likely to spot a few passengers carrying a handi (pot) of mishti-doi; such is the charm of one of the most sought-after sweet-dish. It has helped in putting Bengal on the culinary map of the world. Even though I have grown up having 'mishti doi' for years, I do not recollect it being made at my home or at anyone's home. Every pada (locality) in Kolkata will have a few shops selling it. But outside Bengal, it is a delicacy, which many miss. Though a bit tricky to make, but you would love every mouthful of this most famous Bengali dish when you try making it at home.

Ingredients

½ litre milk, boiled till reduced to 1 cup

4 tablespoons sugar

2 tablespoons yogurt

Method

- Heat reduced milk in a pot.
- Add 2 tablespoons sugar and mix well till the sugar dissolves.
- Heat a pan, add 2 tablespoons sugar and 1 teaspoon water and cook, stirring till the sugar caramelises and turns golden.
- Now heat milk in the pot again, add the caramel and stir it for ½ minute.
- Let it cool. Add yogurt and mix well. Let it set overnight.
- Chill and serve.

Yield: 2 small bowls ***Preparation Skill Level: Moderate***

Gokul Pithe

Stuffed dumplings deep-fried and dipped in sugar syrup

'Pithe' is home-styled dessert and is usually not found in sweet-meat shops. There is a large variety of 'pithe' made in Bengali homes. The 'pithe' my Didu (granny) made were the best. The 'gokul pithe' she made, simply melted in the mouth within seconds. Every year, during 'poush-sankranti' (harvest season), this divine preparation would be made at our home. Looking back I now realise why the 'gokul-pithe' of yesteryears tasted the way it did. It was all due to the presence of my granny's touch of immense love and care, which is so hard to replicate. I still remember the 'pithe' eating competition I had with my brothers and Tuntu having a strong sweet tooth would always win.

Ingredients

Pithe cover

1 cup refined flour

1 teaspoon baking soda

1 pinch salt

1 teaspoon aniseeds

¼ cup sugar

Oil to deep-fry

Filling

1 cup scraped fresh coconut

1 cup grated jaggery

½ cup *mawa*

Sugar syrup

1 cup sugar + 1 cup water

½ teaspoon green cardamom powder

Method

- Mix flour, baking soda, salt, aniseeds and sugar in a bowl. Add sufficient water and whisk to get a thick and smooth batter.
- Take coconut, jaggery and *mawa* in a pan and cook till all these ingredients have mixed well together and excess moisture has evaporated. Keep aside to cool.
- Cook together sugar, 1 cup water and green cardamom powder in another pan till you get a thick syrup. Keep aside.
- Heat sufficient oil in a *kadai*. Divide the filling mixture into small equal portions and shape them into balls. Dip each ball in the batter so that they are well coated. Slide them into hot oil and deep-fry till golden brown.
- Drain and dip them in the sugar syrup for 1 hour.

Serves: 4-6 ***Preparation Skill Level: Moderate***

Patishapta

Rolled crêpes with coconut-jaggery filling

This is a Bengali version of the French crêpe. 'Patishapta' is a member of the 'pithe' family. This 'pithe' was always made at our home along with some other varieties on the very auspicious 'makar-sankranti' day, which usually falls in the middle of January. I regard this day as the world's pithe-day. Remember my mother separating a batch from the prepared heap of 'patishaptas' to dip them in kheer (thickened milk). I would jokingly call the divine tasting kheer soaked patishaptas as 'kheer-shapta'.

Ingredients

Crêpe batter

1 cup refined flour

¼ cup semolina

1½ cups milk

A pinch of salt

2 green cardamoms, powdered

3½ tablespoons sugar

Crêpe filling

1 cup scraped fresh coconut

1 cup grated jaggery

½ cup *mawa*

Method

- Whisk together flour, semolina, milk, salt and green cardamom powder in a bowl till you get a smooth batter. Rest the batter for 1 hour. Add sugar and mix well.
- Cook coconut, jaggery and *mawa* in a pan till everything comes together and the excess liquid dries up. Keep aside this mixture to cool.
- Heat a non-stick skillet. Pour a ladleful of batter, swirl the pan in a circular motion to get perfectly round shaped crêpe. Place 1 tablespoon of filling in the shape of a cylinder on one end of the crêpe.
- Roll the crêpe ensuring that the filling is completely enclosed.
- Serve warm.

Yield: 10-12 pieces ***Preparation Skill Level: Moderate***

Doodh Puli

Jaggery and coconut stuffed dumpling poached in milk sauce

This delicacy marked the onset of the winter and the harvest season. During this time, our neighbourhood would bear a familiar festive smell of 'pithe' and 'puli' being prepared. My grandmother strictly monitored the preparation of this dish as even a tad bit of over or under cooking could ruin it.

Ingredients

Filling

½ cup scraped fresh coconut

½ cup jaggery

Outer casing

1 cup rice flour

½ teaspoon salt

2 cups water

2 teaspoons sugar

1 teaspoon oil

Milk sauce

1 litre milk

½ cup condensed milk

¼ teaspoon cardamom powder

Method

- Heat a pan, add coconut and jaggery, mix and cook till the moisture evaporates and the mixture becomes thick. Keep aside.
- Boil 2 cups water in another pan. Add rice flour, salt, sugar and oil and cook, stirring continuously, ensuring that no lumps form. The mixture should form a thick mass. Knead well while hot till you get a smooth dough. (Be careful with this step, as the dough has to be quickly worked upon while really hot.)
- Divide the dough into equal portions. Stuff each portion with the coconut filling ensuring that the filling is completely enclosed. These are *puli pithe*.
- For the milk sauce, boil milk in a third pan till it reduces to half. Add condensed milk and cardamom powder and mix well.
- Add the *puli pithe* and cook for approximately ½ minute. (Overcooking will make the *pithes* hard.)

Chef's Tips

Instead of poaching in milk sauce, the puli pithes can be steamed. Puli pithes are best enjoyed with nolen gur.

Serves: 4-6 ***Preparation Skill Level: Moderate***

FOREIGN
Influence

British & Anglo-Indian Influence

JOLOJOG & JOLKHABAR (Small Bites)

'Jolojog', the small bites, are popular even as snacks at teatime inspired by the British tea culture. The 'chop-cutlet' loving Bengalis owe these delicious array of jolkhabar to the British and Jew settlers.

Dimer Devil

Crumb-fried egg and potato cutlets

This preparation is quite similar to the authentic British scotch eggs which has mince meat covered whole boiled eggs that are crumb-fried! It is nothing like the English "devilled egg" excepting its name! While inspired from the classic egg preparation, it has been adapted and Indianised with potatoes and spices. This dish featured in our school canteen menu. As soon as the recess bell would ring, I would run to the canteen to have these tasty deep-fried morsels spending all the frugal pocket money I used to get.

Ingredients

4 eggs, hard boiled and peeled

1½ cups boiled and mashed potatoes

1 tablespoon mustard oil

½ cup sliced onions

1 teaspoon ginger paste

1 teaspoon turmeric powder

1 teaspoon red chilli powder

1 teaspoon cumin powder

1 teaspoon coriander powder

Salt to taste

Sugar to taste

1 teaspoon roasted cumin powder

Oil to deep-fry

1 egg, beaten

1 cup breadcrumbs

Method

- Heat mustard oil in a pan. Add onions and sauté till light brown.
- Add ginger paste and mix well.
- Add turmeric powder, chilli powder, cumin powder and coriander powder and mix well. Add potatoes and keep sautéing till the mixture comes together and changes colour.

- Add salt, sugar and roasted cumin powder. The potato mixture is now ready.
- Halve the eggs vertically. Take a lime-sized portion of the potato mixture on your palm and spread. Place a halved egg on it and coat it completely with the potato mixture. Repeat the process with the remaining halved eggs.
- Heat sufficient oil for deep-frying. Dip the potato coated eggs in the beaten egg and then roll them in breadcrumbs.
- Gently slide them into hot oil and deep-fry on medium heat till they are golden brown. Drain on absorbent paper. Serve hot.

Note: *In some places 'dimer devil' is made with mince and potato filling. The above recipe with only potato filling is also known as 'dimer chop'.*

Serves: 4-6 ***Preparation Skill Level: Moderate***

Macher Chop

Crumb fried fish cutlets

Among the many influences that the British gave us in their 200-year reign, the 'chop' preparation is very popular. Anywhere in the world, the word 'chop' would normally mean 'cut-of-a-meat'. However, in Bengal, it typically means fish, meat or vegetables, crumb-fried. It is similar to cutlet preparations, which you may have had. I can never forget that familiar whiff of appetising aroma that rose from the local roadside snack counters every evening around 5 pm. This not-so-subtle reminder that it was snack time brought on the hunger pangs without fail.

Ingredients

2-3 large pieces of fish, boiled and deboned

2 medium potatoes, boiled, peeled and mashed

1 tablespoon oil + to deep-fry

1 tablespoon finely chopped onion

1 teaspoon ginger-garlic paste

½ teaspoon finely chopped green chilli

1 teaspoon turmeric powder

1 teaspoon red chilli powder

1 teaspoon cumin powder

1 teaspoon chopped cashewnuts or peanuts

1 teaspoon raisins

1 teaspoon chopped fresh coriander leaves

1 teaspoon sugar

Salt to taste

1 teaspoon *garam masala* powder

⅓ cup refined flour + for dusting

1 cup breadcrumbs

1 egg, beaten

Method

- Heat oil in a pan. Add onion and sauté till translucent. Add ginger-garlic paste, green chilli, turmeric powder, red chilli powder and cumin powder and mix well.
- Add boiled and deboned fish and mashed potatoes and mix everything well. Add cashewnuts and raisins and mix.
- Add coriander leaves and mix. Add sugar, salt and *garam masala* powder and mix well. Set aside to cool.

- Heat sufficient oil in a *kadai*. Spread flour and breadcrumbs in two different plates. Divide the mixture into equal portions and shape them into balls. Roll them in flour. Then dip them in beaten egg and finally coat them with breadcrumbs.
- Deep-fry these chops/cutlets in hot oil on medium heat till golden brown on all sides. Drain on absorbent paper. Serve hot.

Chef's Tips

- *For vegetarians, instead of fish, use mocha (banana blossoms) to prepare mochar-chop (banana-blossom cutlets).*
- *Another non-vegetarian variation: Instead of fish, use mutton mince to make mangsher chop (mutton cutlets).*

Serves: 4-6 ***Preparation Skill Level: Moderate***

Kobiraji Cutlet

Cutlet, usually made of prawn, covered in egg net

'Kobiraji', the name seems to have emerged from the word "coverage". The dish is a juicy cutlet on the inside with a coating of lacy fried egg on the outside. When I was young I remember going down to the Shyambazar-crossing for evening walks with my grandfather. After the walk we would regularly have Prawn-Kobiraji from a food stall called Allen's Kitchen. This tiny place has been serving the delicacy for more than 80 years. Since I don't have my beloved grandfather's company any longer, nor do I live in Kolkata, I figured out a way to treat myself to this mouth-watering delicacy, in my own kitchen. Each time I prepare 'Kobiraji', it gives me an opportunity to reminisce about my childhood.

Ingredients

4 jumbo prawns, cleaned, deveined, head removed but tail intact

1 teaspoon ginger paste

1 teaspoon garlic paste

1 teaspoon green chilli paste

Salt to taste

1 teaspoon lemon juice

5 eggs

Oil to deep-fry

1 cup breadcrumbs

1 teaspoon cornflour

Method

- Flatten the prawns with a meat mallet.
- Marinate the prawns with ginger paste, garlic paste, green chilli paste, salt and lemon juice for 1 hour.
- Beat 2 eggs in a bowl. Beat the remaining 3 eggs well with a pinch of salt in another bowl.
- Dip the flattened, marinated prawns in 2 beaten eggs first and then coat them with breadcrumbs. Shape into proper cutlets leaving the tail intact. Deep-fry in hot oil till golden. Drain on absorbent paper.
- To make the netlike cover on the cutlets, add cornflour to 3 beaten eggs and mix well till smooth.
- Dip fingers in this mixture, lift the hand and make quick vertical hand movements above the hot oil.

- A net-like structure will form on the oil. Carefully place the fried cutlet in the middle of the prepared egg-net.
- Cover the cutlet with the egg-net from all sides to envelope completely. Drain on absorbent paper. Serve hot.
- The cutlet should be fully covered by the egg net hence the name *Kobiraji* or 'coverage' cutlet.

Serves: 2-4 | ***Preparation Skill Level: Difficult***

NANA-ROKOM BHAAT (Miscellaneous Rice-Based Preparation)

Bengalis love their rice. 'Bhaat' (rice) is consumed at any time of the day, be it breakfast, lunch or dinner. Dishes like 'pish pash', the one pot Anglo-Indian meal, were well amalgamated into Bengali cuisine by the rice loving clan.

Pish Pash

A mushy pilaf made with meat and milk

Total comfort food! An Anglo-Indian one-pot delicacy, it is the Bengali answer to the Italian Risotto. This dish is bland and usually termed as food for the sick because of its cold busting and immunity boosting power. It is similar to chicken soup, known as Jewish penicillin and I know why! I remember my mother making this often whenever I felt a little under the weather.

Ingredients

1 cup rice (preferably *Gobindo bhog* rice), soaked for 15 minutes and drained

2 tablespoons split red lentil

250 grams mutton pieces

2 tablespoons butter

1 bay leaf

1 inch cinnamon

3-4 cloves

2-3 green cardamoms

½ teaspoon ginger paste

½ teaspoon garlic paste

2 medium onions, quartered

1 medium potato, peeled and halved

Optional vegetables: A few carrot cubes, French beans and peas

2 green chillies

Salt to taste

1 teaspoon sugar

3-4 tablespoons milk

2 tablespoons deep-fried onions, to garnish

Chopped fresh coriander leaves, to garnish

Method

- Heat butter in a pressure cooker. Add bay leaf, cinnamon, cloves, cardamoms, ginger paste and garlic paste and sauté for few seconds.

- Add onions, lentils, potato, veggies if using, mutton, rice, green chillies, salt, sugar and milk. Add 3 cups water and pressure-cook till the mutton is tender.
- Sprinkle fried onion and coriander leaves and serve hot. (Optional)

Chef's Tips

To make it vegetarian, substitute mutton with various vegetables like carrots, beans, capsicum, paneer/tofu, etc.

Serves: 2-3 ***Preparation Skill Level: Easy***

British influence on 'murgi' (chicken) and 'mangsho' (meat) preparations is characterised by creamy sauces, restrained use of spices and techniques such as baking.

Daak-Bungalow Chicken

Type of chicken curry from the Raj (i.e. British) era

The story of the 'daak-bungalow' chicken goes all the way down to the colonial era - the time of the British Raj. The Sahebs, as the then British officials were called, used to frequently tour from one place to another. Every time they stopped by at a rest house or a daak-bungalow, the caretakers of the transit homes would cook them their meals. This is where the origins of this masterpiece lie. The caretakers were the ones who came up with this creation. They used chicken, fried eggs and potato to prepare this dish, providing a wholesome meal to their guests.

Ingredients

750 grams chicken, cut into 8 pieces on the bone

1 cup paste (made from 2 medium onions, 2 inch ginger, 4-5 garlic cloves, 2 medium tomatoes and 2 green chillies)

½ cup yogurt

1 teaspoon red chilli powder

1 teaspoon cumin powder

1 teaspoon turmeric powder

1 teaspoon *garam masala* powder

4 tablespoons mustard oil

Salt to taste

1 teaspoon sugar

2 medium onions, sliced

2-3 eggs, hard boiled and peeled

2 medium potatoes boiled, peeled and halved

2 tablespoons *ghee*

2-3 green chillies

Handful of fresh coriander leaves, chopped

Method

- Mix chicken with onion-tomato paste, yogurt, red chilli powder, cumin powder, ½ teaspoon turmeric powder, *garam masala* powder, 2 tablespoons mustard oil, salt and sugar in a bowl and keep the bowl in the refrigerator to marinate, preferably overnight.

- Heat 2 tablespoons mustard oil in a pressure cooker. Fry 2 tablespoons of sliced onions till pink. Add the marinated chicken into a pressure cooker and cook under pressure till 2-3 whistles are given out.
- Apply ½ teaspoon turmeric powder on the eggs and potatoes.
- Heat 2 tablespoons *ghee* in a pan. Add turmeric coated potatoes and eggs and shallow-fry till red. Drain and keep aside. Add rest of the onions and green chillies to the *ghee* remaining in the pan, and sauté till onions are golden.
- Garnish the chicken with onions, chillies, eggs, potatoes and coriander leaves and serve hot.

Serves: 4-6 ***Preparation Skill Level: Moderate***

Chicken Stew

A light, aromatic chicken and vegetable preparation

This dish has a British-cum-Irish influence. "Chitto-babur Dokaan" at Decker's Lane is supposed to make this dish the best, and perhaps they are doing so for almost a century. The chicken stew with toast at this road-side stall is such a hit that even today, people queue up for it! I always associate chicken stew to be served when one is ill. It's bland but very healthy. Even today when anyone in my family falls ill, this is my antibiotic to rejuvenate them – chicken soup for the soul, as they say!

Ingredients

4-5 pieces of chicken on the bone
1 teaspoon oil
1 tablespoon butter
2 cloves
2 green cardamoms
2 one-inch cinnamon sticks
1-2 bay leaves
1 medium onion, sliced
2 tablespoons minced garlic
½ cup carrot cubes
½ cup ½-inch pieces of French beans
2 medium potatoes, halved
Salt to taste
Black pepper powder to taste
Few whole peppercorns
½ cup milk
1 tablespoon cornflour or whole wheat flour
Handful of fresh coriander leaves, chopped

Method

- Heat oil and butter in a pressure cooker. Lightly crush cloves, cardamoms, cinnamon and bay leaves and add to the cooker and sauté for 30 seconds.
- Add onion and garlic; sauté for 1 minute. Add carrots, French beans and potatoes and sauté for 2-3 minutes. Add chicken and continue to sauté for 2-3 minutes. Add salt and pepper powder, whole peppercorns and mix well. Add enough warm water to fully cover chicken and vegetables.
- Close the pressure cooker and cook under pressure for 5 minutes on high heat.
- When the pressure reduces, open the lid of the cooker and add milk mixed with cornflour or wheat flour and cook for 2-3 minutes.

Note: *This dish can also be made with mutton or vegetables.*

Serves: 2-3 ***Preparation Skill Level: Easy***

MISHTIMUKH (Dessert)

Bengalis are known for their sweet tooth. Bengali sweets or 'mishti', though are of unending varieties, did not prevent them from adapting goodies from others including the Anglo-Indians. Bengal received innate influences of the Raj era in several ways including its cuisine. The Christmas cakes, bakes and puddings have a strong British-colonial influence.

Christmas Cake

The true British influence in their erstwhile Indian capital is the sombre celebration on the 'boro-din' (the big day), which is the other name for Christmas. The one product which denotes this day in an otherwise Hindu State, is a special variety of cake interspersed with loads of raisins and 'petha' (ash gourd candy). Incidentally petha perhaps is not used anywhere else in the world in these type of cakes. Even after so many years, whenever I visit Kolkata during the winters, I make sure I pick up the cake at the Jewish bakers 'Nahoum' in New Market, which still makes the Christmas cake exactly the same way as it used to be when I was a kid.

Ingredients

1 cup refined flour

1 teaspoon baking powder

1 teaspoon baking soda

1 cup almond meal

100 grams butter + to grease

½ cup honey

½ cup orange juice

1 teaspoon grated orange zest

1 teaspoon cinnamon powder

2 tablespoon cocoa powder

1 cup brown sugar

6-7 tablespoons rum

1 cup chopped candied orange peel

4-5 tablespoons raisins

4 tablespoons black raisins/sultanas

1 cup chopped prunes

1 cup chopped candied ash gourd (*petha*)

3 eggs

Method

- Preheat the oven to 180°C. Grease a baking tin with butter.
- Heat a pan. Add butter, honey and orange juice and mix.

- Add orange zest, cinnamon powder, cocoa powder and brown sugar and mix. Add rum, orange peel, raisins, sultanas and prunes and mix.
- Boil this mixture and add the candied ash gourd and mix. Keep aside. (Some people soak the raisins and sultanas in rum for a month. The rum soaked raisins give a unique flavour to the cake.)
- Beat the eggs in a bowl, add flour, baking powder, baking soda and almond meal and mix well. Add fruit peel and alcohol mixture and mix well.
- Pour the mixture into the greased cake tin. Bake in the preheated oven for 1 hour. Take the tin out of the oven and let it cool down to room temperature.
- Gently dislodge the cake from the tin, slice and serve.

Serves: 6-8 ***Preparation Skill Level: Moderate***

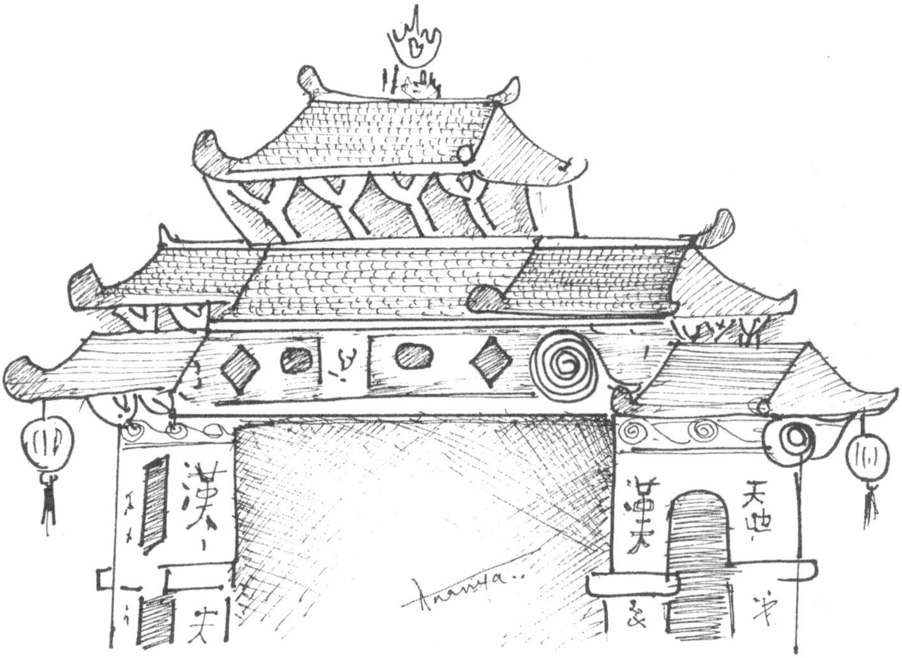

Chinese Influence

JOLOJOG & JOLKHABAR (Small Bites)

'Jolojog' means tiny bites, which can be had at any time, including as snacks, at breakfast or at teatime. World over the well-known 'Dimsum', usually served in steamer baskets, is a Chinese-styled snack. 'Momo' a popular offshoot of 'Dimsum' and is immensely liked in Bengal. Freshly made 'Chowmein' is the all time favourite 'jolkhabar' in Kolkata, which can be had on the move.

Chowmein

Stir-fried noodles

While the world over, noodles are the most popular part of the Chinese cuisine; this noodle dish is referred to as 'Chowmein' both in Kolkata and in China. 'Chow' implying stir-fried and 'mein' meaning noodles.

Ingredients

1 packet (200 grams) noodles

4-5 tablespoons oil

1 teaspoon ginger paste

1 teaspoon garlic paste

1 cup chopped onions

2 chopped green chillies

1 cup finely sliced mixed vegetables (carrot, cabbage and capsicum)

1 tablespoon soy sauce

1 tablespoon red chilli sauce

A pinch of sugar

Salt to taste

Method

- Boil the noodles in plenty of water in a large pot till al dente. Drain and wash under cold running water to cool completely. Drain again, apply 2 teaspoons oil and set aside.
- Heat 2 tablespoons oil in pan. Toss the noodles till the oil coats them well. Drain and keep them aside.
- Heat the remaining oil in the same pan, add ginger paste and garlic paste and sauté for a minute. Add onions, green chillies, noodles and mixed vegetables. Toss well for 2 minutes, stirring vigorously on high heat.
- Add soy sauce, chilli sauce, sugar and salt. Mix well and serve hot.

Serves: 3-4 ***Preparation Skill Level: Easy***

Tangra-Style American Chopsuey

Deep-fried noodle preparation

'American Chopsuey' is a popular New England pasta and beef dish. But the recipe here is an outcome of a fusion of Chinese influence mingling with the Anglo-Indian taste. Fried noodles served in a distinctive style, pepped up with sweet and sour sauce and topped with a fried egg. It is so typical, that till some years ago it was well-nigh impossible to even locate it outside Kolkata. However in the recent years it is available in most Indian cities where it has become very popular. I still remember Munia, my uncle, used to take me out for a treat whenever I fared well in my exams – and it used to be to Park Street, the centre-point of top-quality restaurants – and my most sought after dish was the tangy 'American Chopsuey'.

Ingredients

1 packet (200 grams) noodles, boiled as per instruction on the packet

2 tablespoons + 6 teaspoons oil + to deep-fry

6 eggs

1 medium onion, sliced

1 teaspoon minced garlic

½ cup chopped French beans

½ cup chopped carrots

½ cup shredded cabbage

1 medium green capsicum, sliced

½ cup chicken mince

2 tablespoons cornflour mixed with ½ cup water

½ teaspoon white pepper powder

½ teaspoon black pepper powder

½ cup tomato ketchup

1 tablespoon soy sauce

1 teaspoon sugar

Salt to taste

Method

- Heat sufficient oil and deep-fry the noodles till crisp. Drain on absorbent paper.
- Beat 2 eggs in a bowl. Heat 2 teaspoons oil in a pan, add the beaten eggs and cook stirring continuously till they scramble. Transfer into a clean bowl and keep aside.
- Heat 1 teaspoon oil in the same pan and prepare one fried egg (sunny side up). Repeat this process and prepare 3 more fried eggs. Keep them aside.

- To make the sauce, heat 2 tablespoon oil in a pan. Add onion, garlic, French beans, carrots, cabbage and capsicum and sauté for 3 minutes. Add 2 cups water and chicken mince and cook for 2 minutes or till the chicken gets cooked.
- Add cornflour mixture, white and black pepper powders and mix well.
- Add tomato ketchup, soy sauce and sugar. Add salt and mix well. Cook till the gravy thickens. Add scrambled eggs and mix well. Keep aside.
- To assemble, for each portion put some crisply fried noodles in a serving bowl. Drizzle some sauce over them and place 1 fried egg on top. Serve immediately.

Serves: 4 ***Preparation Skill Level: Moderate***

Tangra-Style Chilli Chicken

Indo-Chinese chicken preparation

'Bengali Chinese' is quite different from what the rest of the world serves as Chinese. Chilli chicken today is very popular in the Indian subcontinent. But the 'tangra' chilli chicken is not submerged with thick corn flour gravy like everywhere else. In 'tangra region', (China town in eastern Kolkata) there are countless eateries serving the mouth-watering Chinese preparations for years. This cuisine is not solely restricted to a single community anymore - a legacy that has penetrated through numerous households. As the Chinese opened their restaurants, they spiced up the bland Cantonese sauce with sliced chillies and other ingredients. They also came up with names such as 'Chilli Chicken' to attract customers. I have grown up having chilli chicken. It somehow never feels that it is a dish from a foreign cuisine. For me it is as integral a part of Bengali cuisine as 'mangshor jhol' is. Believe it or not, you cannot find 'chilli chicken' in China!

Ingredients

1 cup small pieces of boneless chicken

4 green chillies, chopped

1 tablespoon green chilli paste

2 tablespoons soy sauce

1½ tablespoons minced garlic

1 egg, beaten

3 tablespoons cornflour + 1 tablespoon flour

2 tablespoons oil

1 tablespoon minced ginger

1 tablespoon finely chopped onion

1 tablespoon chopped green capsicum

Salt to taste

1 teaspoon black pepper powder

1 tablespoon chopped spring onion

1 tablespoon chopped fresh coriander leaves

Method

- Take chicken pieces in a bowl, add 1 tablespoon soy sauce, green chilli paste, ½ tablespoon minced garlic and egg and mix well. Add 2 tablespoons cornflour + 1 tablespoon flour and mix well. Keep covered in a refrigerator to marinate for 30 minutes.
- Take remaining cornflour in a small bowl, add ¼ cup water and mix well to make slurry.
- Heat oil in a pan, add chicken and sauté till the pieces are lightly coloured. Drain on absorbent paper.

- In the oil remaining in the pan add remaining minced garlic, minced ginger, chopped green chillies and onion and sauté well. Add capsicum and remaining soy sauce. Mix well together.
- Add salt and black pepper powder and mix. Add the chicken pieces and toss well.
- Garnish with spring onions and coriander leaves. Serve hot.

Note: *Typical tangra-style chilli chicken is also served dry, where the cornflour slurry is not added to prepare any gravy. It is extremely popular with alcoholic beverages.*

Serves: 2-3 | *Preparation Skill Level: Moderate*

Momo (Tibetan)

Steamed stuffed flour dumplings

Momos are little packets of sheer glee, filled with cabbage or minced meat, steamed or fried and eaten with tangy momo sauce or chilli garlic sauce. They have become one of Kolkata's most loved snacks lately. They are healthy, yummy, easy-to-gobble and definitely pocket-friendly. With the 14th Dalai Lama fleeing to India, many Tibetans settled in the eastern parts of India and brought some of their food with them. When I was a child, there were hardly any momo-shops in Kolkata. I sampled my first momo in Darjeeling. Nowadays, this Tibetan import is available all over Kolkata and is competing with the city's traditional staples.

Ingredients

Dough for momo

1 cup refined flour

A pinch of salt

1 tablespoon oil

Filling

½ cup chicken mince

½ cup finely chopped onion

½ cup finely chopped spring onion

½ cup finely chopped fresh coriander leaves

1 tablespoon minced garlic

1 teaspoon minced ginger

2-3 green chillies, minced

1 egg

Salt to taste

Black pepper powder to taste

Method

- To make the filling, take chicken mince in a large mixing bowl. Add onion, spring onion, coriander leaves, garlic, ginger, green chillies, egg, salt and black pepper powder and mix well. Cover the bowl and keep in the refrigerator to marinate for at least 1 hour.
- To make the momo wrapper, combine flour, salt and enough warm water in a bowl and knead to a pliable dough. (The process should take about 10 minutes). Cover and let it stand for at least 15 minutes.
- Knead well again and incorporate 1 tablespoon oil into the dough. Divide the dough into equal small marble sized balls.

- Roll out each ball into a small disc, place 1 tablespoon of filling mixture in the centre, pleat the edges and bring them together to the centre. Twist and pinch them to seal the dumplings.
- Heat sufficient water in a steamer and grease the steamer rack well. Arrange momos on the rack and steam for 8-10 minutes. Serve hot with a hot and tangy sauce.

Momo Sauce

Blend together 1 medium roughly chopped tomato, 2-3 garlic cloves, 3-4 dried red chillies that have been soaked in hot water, 1 tablespoon cashewnuts or peanuts, 1 teaspoon sugar and salt to taste, to a paste. Transfer the paste into a serving bowl. Heat 1 tablespoon oil and pour on top of the paste. Mix well. Serve with the momos.

Serves: 3-4 ***Preparation Skill Level: Moderate***

NANA-ROKOM BHAAT (Miscellaneous Rice-Based Preparation)

'Bhaat' or rice is grown abundantly in Bengal. No wonder it is consumed almost in all meals. Bengalis have concocted a tasty variance of the rice preparation – the 'Chinese-style fried rice'. It is now well accepted by the rice-loving Bengali households.

Fried Rice

Stir-fried rice with vegetables and /or meat

Chinese cuisine is truly one of the most adaptive of world cuisines. While fried-rice is generally made with fragrant rice, the Bengali-Chinese version uses 'sheddho-chaal' (parboiled rice), which is not used elsewhere. Even today, tired from the day's work, when one has to rustle up something quick and satisfying, I make Chinese fried rice, usually from leftover rice and whatever veggies and or chicken and eggs found in the refrigerator.

Ingredients

1 cup cooked rice

2 tablespoons oil

1 egg

1 tablespoon chopped onion

1 tablespoon chopped garlic

1 tablespoon chopped ginger

1 tablespoon green chilli paste

1 cup chopped mixed vegetables

1 teaspoon black pepper powder

Salt to taste

1 tablespoon soy sauce

1 tablespoon chopped fresh coriander leaves

1 tablespoon chopped spring onions

Method

- Heat oil in a pan. Add egg and cook stirring till it scrambles. Transfer it onto a plate and keep aside.
- In the oil remaining in the pan, add onion, garlic, ginger, green chilli paste and mixed vegetables and sauté for a while.
- Then add rice, black pepper powder, salt and soy sauce. Add scrambled egg and mix well. Garnish with coriander leaves and spring onions and serve hot.

Chef's Tips

To make it vegetarian, omit the egg.

Serves: 1-2 ***Preparation Skill Level: Easy***

MAACH (Fish)

'Maach' or fish is almost synonymous with Bengal and Bengalis. It is more of an emotion than food for most Bongs. Over the years, various techniques and influence in preparing fish have found their way into Bengal homes. It is but natural that the popular Chinese-styled chilli fish and batter-fried prawns are served during many Bengali get-togethers.

Kolkata-Style Chilli Fish

Fish with soya and chilli, prepared by Chinese settlers in Kolkata

Bengalis love fish in any form, and better if it is served hot and tangy. The Chinese settlers in Kolkata figured out the innate weakness of the Bong tongues. The Chinese twisted and turned their own recipe to produce a delicious variant which does not resemble anything available in their own homes back in China. Beer and chilli fish is a great way to unwind and have a heated 'adda' (chit-chat) on anything from football to food.

Ingredients

Batter fried fish

400 grams fish fillet (any firm white flesh fish like *bhetki* or *basa*)

1 coarsely grated onion

1 teaspoon ginger paste

1 teaspoon garlic paste

2 -3 green chillies, minced

1 egg

Salt to taste

3 tablespoons cornflour

3 tablespoon refined flour

Oil to deep-fry

Gravy

3-4 tablespoons oil

1 teaspoon sugar

1 medium onion, diced

1 teaspoon minced ginger

1½ teaspoons minced garlic

4-5 green chillies slit

1 medium green capsicum, cubed

Salt to taste

2-3 tablespoons dark soy sauce

2 teaspoons green chilli sauce

1 tablespoon tomato ketchup

2 tablespoons vinegar

1 tablespoon cornflour mixed with
2 tablespoons water

1 tablespoon thin strips of spring onion

Method

- Marinate the fish pieces with onion, ginger paste, garlic paste and chillies for 1 hour.
- Beat the egg in a bowl, add salt, cornflour, refined flour and a little water and mix well to make a thick batter. Add the fish pieces and mix until all the pieces and well coated with the batter.
- Heat sufficient oil and deep-fry the batter coated fish till golden brown. *(These tiny fish bites are perfect as starters!)* Drain on absorbent paper and keep aside.
- For the gravy, heat oil in a wok, add sugar and let it caramelise. Add onion and sauté for 2-3 minutes. Add ginger and 1 teaspoon garlic and sauté for another 2-3 minutes.
- Add chillies and capsicum and sauté on high heat for a few minutes. Add salt to taste. Add dark soy sauce, green chilli sauce, tomato ketchup and vinegar and mix well. Add cornflour slurry with some water and mix well. Cook till the gravy thickens. Add ½ teaspoon garlic. Add the fried fish and toss in the gravy.
- Garnish with spring onions strips and serve hot.

Serves: 3-4 ***Preparation Skill Level: Moderate***

Tangra-Style Golden Fried Prawns

Crispy batter-fried prawns served in Chinatown, Kolkata

Tangra is the Chinatown of Kolkata. The Chinese settled in Tangra have enmeshed themselves so much with the local culture, that they even have a Hindu Goddess (Kali) temple there. To take the cultural confluence a bit further, they kept innovating on their own cuisine, to suit the local Bengali palates. The golden fried prawns make the fish-loving Bengalis enjoy their favourite prawns in Chinese avatar.

Ingredients

8-10 large prawns, cleaned and deveined

Salt to taste

White pepper powder to taste

1 cup cornflour

1 cup refined flour

1 teaspoon baking soda

Oil to deep-fry

Stir-fry

2 tablespoons oil

2 -3 tablespoons minced green chillies

2 tablespoons thin strips of ginger

2 tablespoons chopped spring onions

2 tablespoons freshly chopped coriander leaves

Method

- Apply salt and pepper powder to prawns and keep them aside to marinate for 30 minutes.
- Combine the cornflour and refined flour in a bowl. Add baking soda and salt. Add sufficient water and whisk well till you get a batter of smooth pouring consistency.
- Heat sufficient oil in a deep pan. Dip each prawn in the batter and deep-fry until golden. Drain on absorbent paper and keep aside.
- Heat oil in a wok, add green chillies, ginger strips, spring onions and coriander leaves and sauté. Add the golden prawns and sauté for 1-2 minutes.
- Serve hot.

Serves: 4-6 ***Preparation Skill Level: Easy***

Mughlai
Influence

JOLOJOG & JOLKHABAR (Small Bites)

'Jolojog' or small bites are preparations that can be had at any time. In Mughlai-style Bengali preparations, kebabs are perfect as a 'jolojog'. 'Kathi-rolls' stuffed with kebabs are an all-time favourite 'jholkhabar' for Bengalis.

Chicken Roll

Kebabs wrapped in eggy parathas to make cylindrical rolls

When you are hungry and find yourself on the streets of Kolkata, the best option for a quick bite are freshly made rolls. This popular street food was a staple at my home, though the kebabs my Mom prepared were made in a pan instead of the traditional 'tandoor' which is usually commercially available. I could happily have this for breakfast, lunch, dinner or evening snacks. Nizam's restaurant in Kolkata invented the first rolls. It is colloquially known as 'kathi-rolls' as the kababs are skewered on a thin skewer or kathi. It has now become the source of joy in the 'City of Joy'.

Ingredients

Kathi kababs

1 cup small cubes of boneless chicken

2 tablespoons yogurt

2 teaspoons *tandoori masala* (optional)

1 tablespoon oil

1 tablespoon sliced onion

2 tablespoons chopped green capsicum

1 teaspoon chopped garlic

1 teaspoon chopped ginger

1 tablespoon green chilli paste

Salt to taste

Dough for *parathas*

1 cup refined flour

1 tablespoon oil + to cook

Salt to taste

2 eggs

To assemble

2 tablespoons finely chopped onion

1 tablespoon chopped cucumber

1 teaspoon chopped green chillies

1 teaspoon *chaat masala*

2 teaspoons lemon juice

4 teaspoons tomato ketchup

1 tablespoon chopped fresh coriander leaves

Method

- Take chicken pieces in a large mixing bowl, add yogurt and *tandoori masala* and mix well. Keep the bowl in the refrigerator to marinate for 30-60 minutes.
- Take flour in another large mixing bowl, add oil, salt and sufficient water and knead into a soft dough. Cover with a damp cloth and set aside for 15 minutes.
- To make the *kababs* heat oil in a pan. Add onion, capsicum, garlic and ginger and sauté till fragrant. Add green chilli paste and mix well.
- Add marinated chicken and salt and mix well. Sauté till the chicken is done and the mixture becomes dry.
- Divide the dough into 4 equal portions.
- Dust each ball with a little dry flour and roll out into *parathas*.
- Heat a *tawa* and cook the *parathas*, one at a time, flipping till they are evenly done on both sides.
- Beat eggs with a little salt in a small bowl.
- Heat the *tawa* again and drizzle a little oil on it. Pour ¼ egg mixture on it and place a *paratha* on it.
- Drizzle a little oil all around and cook till the *parathas* turn a golden brown. Repeat this process with the remaining egg mixture and remaining *parathas*.
- Line each serving plate with a piece of aluminium foil. Place a *paratha* on it, put some chicken, onion, cucumber and green chillies on it. Sprinkle *chaat masala*, lemon juice, tomato ketchup and coriander leaves.
- Roll it with aluminum foil and serve.

Note: *These rolls can also be made with mutton, vegetables or cottage cheese.*

Serves: 3-4 ***Preparation Skill Level: Moderate***

NANA-ROKOM BHAAT (Miscellaneous Rice-Based Preparation)

For Bengalis, life without 'bhaat' or rice, is no life. The Mughlai influence has imparted rich flavour and distinctive aroma to rice dishes, which is unanimously loved by the rice-loving clan.

Kolkata Biriyani (Mutton)

Aromatic rice dish popular in Bengal

The Kolkata Biriyani derived its method of cooking from the Awadhi style, with a touch of local taste. It is a combination of hypnotising aroma, the finely flavoured rice and less of spice. Not to forget, the quintessential aloo (potatoes), which is a Bengali trademark in the dish. There are few theories as to why the potatoes were first added to the original recipe. I read somewhere that the economic condition of Bengal at that time did not permit the use of too much meat, hence many substituted meat with boiled eggs and potatoes, making it a pocket-friendly dish. Whereas, Begum Manzilat Fatima, a descendant of Nawab Wajid Ali, who happens to be a friend, said that during those days potato was a new age import by the Portuguese and the erstwhile nawab and his cooks added the exotic, new stuff in their 'biriyani'. While I am not quite sure which version is accurate, what I do know for sure is that the aloo in Kolkata biriyani tastes even better than the meat.

Ingredients

½ kg rice, soaked for 15 minutes and drained

1 kg mutton, cut into large pieces on the bone

2 tablespoons green papaya paste

3-4 boiled medium potatoes

3-4 hardboiled eggs

4 tablespoons mustard oil

1 cup onion-ginger-garlic-tomato paste

1 teaspoon cumin powder

1 tablespoon Kashmiri red-chilli powder

1 cup yogurt

2 tablespoons *Biriyani masala*

2-3 green chillies, chopped

Salt to taste

1 teaspoon sugar

½ teaspoon turmeric powder

4 tablespoons *ghee*

½ cup deep-fried sliced onions

¼ teaspoon rose water

2 drops screwpine water

1 drop *mitha attar*

¼ cup saffron milk (a few saffron strands soaked in ½ cup warm milk and 1 tablespoon butter)

Method

- Marinate the mutton overnight in papaya paste and yogurt.
- Heat 3 tablespoons oil in a pan. Add onion-ginger-garlic-tomato paste and sauté till fragrant. Add cumin powder, Kashmiri red chilli powder and sauté well. Add marinated mutton to the pan.
- Add 1 tablespoon *biriyani masala* and green chillies. Mix well. Cover and cook till the mutton is almost done, around 30 minutes. Add salt and sugar and mix well.
- Heat 1 tablespoon oil in a pan. Apply turmeric powder and salt on the eggs and potatoes and sauté them in hot oil till light golden. Drain and keep aside.
- Cook rice in plenty of water till ¾ done. Drain well.
- Add salt, 2 tablespoons *ghee*, 1 tablespoon *biriyani masala* and a little deep-fried onions to the rice and mix. Add rose water, screw-pine water and *mitha attar* and mix well.
- Place the cooked mutton at the base of a thick bottomed pan. Sprinkle remaining *ghee* on top. Sprinkle half the saffron milk, and half the remaining fried onions on top. Spread the rice on top. Arrange the potatoes and eggs on the rice. Sprinkle the remaining saffron milk and remaining deep-fried onion. Secure the pan with a tight fitting lid.
- Place the whole pan into a larger pan with boiling water and simmer on low heat for 20 minutes. (This method is known as dum or creating steam for the mutton and rice to cook completely).
- Let it stand for 10 minutes. Serve hot.

Note: *This can also be made with mutton, vegetables or cottage cheese.*

Chef's Tips

Veg biriyani can be made substituting chicken with vegetables of choice or paneer.

(Recipe for Biriyani masala:- Grind together 2 tablespoons green cardamoms, 2 tablespoons cinnamon, 2 tablespoons cloves, ¼ teaspoon nutmeg powder, 1 mace blade, ½ tablespoon kabab chini and 2-3 bay leaves to a coarse powder.)

Serves: 6-8 ***Preparation Skill Level: Difficult***

POROTA (Bengali-Style Bread)

Bengalis love 'maida' (refined flour) unlike rest of India where 'atta' is more popular. The Mughlai twist is the use of oodles of butter and ghee as key ingredients, kneaded into a dough, hence creating delicious flaky layers.

Mughlai Porota

Flaky parathas stuffed with keema and egg

Surely not for the faint hearted! A flaky, crispy porota stuffed with mutton mince and eggs. One of these will keep the tummy full all day! I fondly remember our family's Sunday evening treats. My dad would take us to Anadi-Cabin restaurant on Dharmatala Street in Kolkata, one of the pioneers in making 'mughlai porota'. He believed one Sunday meal outside home would give our domestic help a much-desired rest! Needless to say that none of us complained and waited eagerly for Sundays to come.

Ingredients

Dough

1 cup refined flour

3 tablespoons oil

Salt to taste

Filling

250 grams or 1 cup mutton mince, boiled

½ cup chopped onions

1 teaspoon finely minced garlic

2 green chillies, finely chopped

2 tablespoons chopped fresh coriander leaves

2 eggs

Salt to taste

Oil to shallow-fry

Method

- Knead together flour, 1 tablespoon oil, salt with sufficient water to a smooth dough. Pour 2 tablespoons oil on the dough and keep aside to rest for at least 1 hour.
- Mix the mutton mince with onions, garlic, green chillies, coriander leaves and eggs. Add salt and mix again.

- Divide the dough into 4 parts and form balls. Roll out each ball into a very thin rectangle.
- Place 2 tablespoons of the mince mixture in the middle of each rectangle. Spread it evenly in the middle leaving a margin of 4 cms on all sides.
- Fold the uncovered dough from all 4 sides to cover the filled portion to form an envelope. This forms the *porota*.
- Heat a skillet *tawa*, and cook the *porotas*, one at a time.
- Flip, drizzle a little oil on all 4 sides, flip again and drizzle some more oil on all 4 sides. Cook, turning sides, till it is evenly golden on both sides. Serve hot.

Serves: 3-4 ***Preparation Skill Level: Moderate***

TORI-TARKARI (Vegetable Preparation)

Vegetables are part and parcel of any cuisine. Bengali food is no exception. The Mughlai influence however calls for exotic use of spices, dried fruit and nuts to prepare delectable and unique vegetarian and non-vegetarian dishes.

Potoler Dorma

Pointed gourd with a cottage cheese stuffing

Dorma comes from the word 'Dolma' which stands for filling or stuffing. This dish has Middle Eastern and East European connections. Every stuffing-based preparation usually needs a base, and for this dish it is the 'Potol' (pointed gourd). Making this dish is labourious and is often prepared to impress someone. Mashima (my friend's mom) could make it easily for almost all occasions. I always wondered how she could manage this difficult dish in a jiffy. After much cajoling, she spilled the beans. Her secret was, instead of the tedious task of scooping out the raw potol and then stuffing it, she deep-fried the potol first. That made it soft and easy to work on. I feel blessed to keep learning from my elders who are all a storehouse of knowledge. From that day, making 'potoler dorma' became a cakewalk for me!

Ingredients

6-8 pointed gourds (*potol*)
Oil to deep-fry
½ teaspoon turmeric powder
Salt to taste

Stuffing

1 tablespoon *ghee*
½ teaspoon cumin seeds
1 cup grated cottage cheese
3-4 cashewnuts, chopped
8-10 raisins
1 teaspoon sugar
1 teaspoon *garam masala* powder
Salt to taste

Gravy

1 tablespoon chopped cashewnuts
1 medium tomato
1 medium onion
½ inch ginger
1 teaspoon chopped green chillies
2 tablespoons mustard oil
½ teaspoon turmeric powder
1 teaspoon red chilli powder
1 teaspoon cumin powder
Sugar to taste
Salt to taste
1 teaspoon *garam masala* powder

Method

- To make the stuffing, heat *ghee* in a pan, add cumin seeds and sauté till they change colour.
- Add cottage cheese, cashewnuts, raisins, sugar, *garam masala* powder and salt. Mix and cook till everything comes together. Keep aside and cool.
- Heat sufficient oil in a *kadai*.
- Peel the gourds and keep in a bowl. Add ½ teaspoon turmeric powder and salt and mix. Deep-fry the whole gourds till they are soft. Drain on absorbent paper and keep aside to cool.
- Slit one end of the gourds and scoop out the seeds and flesh creating a hollow.
- Stuff each gourd with the cottage cheese stuffing and keep aside on a plate.
- For the gravy grind together cashewnuts, tomato, onion, ginger and green chillies to a smooth paste.
- Heat mustard oil in a pan, add the paste, ½ teaspoon turmeric powder, chilli powder and cumin powder, sugar to taste, salt and keep sautéing till the oil leaves the *masala* and the gravy thickens.
- Add the stuffed gourds to the gravy and simmer till they are soft. Sprinkle *garam masala* powder. Serve hot.

Note: *The gourds can also be stuffed with chicken, mutton or prawn mince.*

Chef's Tips

- *Traditionally the raw gourds are slit and seeds are cored out thereby making a hollow inside; then it is stuffed and deep-fried. But deep-frying before stuffing makes it less tedious.*
- *If you want to avoid deep-frying, microwave the peeled gourds for 5 minutes. This will make them soft and easy to core and stuff them thereby making the dish considerably less oily.*

Serves: 4-6 ***Preparation Skill Level: Difficult***

MAACH (Fish)

It is a no brainer that Bengalis love their fish or 'maach' more than a lot of things in life. It does not come as a surprise that 'maach' or fish has found its way into Bengali homes in several methods and influences. Some of the Mughlai and Bangladeshi-styled fish preparations call for rich and elaborate cooking techniques with mouth-watering outcome.

Chitol Petir Kaliya

Spicy, rich and festive preparation of knife fish

This dish is spectacular to look at given the size and presentation of the chitol (knife fish). Unlike the 'jhol' which is usually a daily Bengali dish, the 'kaliya' has a rich gravy that is perfect for special occasions. The 'kaliya' can also be prepared with 'rohu', 'katla' or 'bhetki' fish. This used to be a "jamai shosti" (son-in-law's day) special along with an array of delicacies prepared by my granny for my dad! The largest 'chitolpeti', the biggest lobster for 'chingri malai curry' along with a gigantic sized 'rajbhog' (giant rosogolla) used to be served to impress the 'jamai'!

Ingredients

½ kg knife fish (*chitol maach*), cut into chunks

Salt to taste

1 teaspoon turmeric powder

4-5 tablespoons mustard oil

2 cloves

2 green cardamoms

½ inch cinnamon stick

1-2 bay leaves

½ teaspoon cumin seeds

2 tablespoons onion paste

½ teaspoon ginger paste

2 tablespoons tomato paste

1 teaspoon red chilli powder

1 teaspoon cumin powder

½ teaspoon coriander powder

½ cup yogurt, beaten

1 tablespoon cashewnut paste

Sugar to taste

1 teaspoon *desi ghee*

½ teaspoon *garam masala* powder

1 tablespoon chopped fresh coriander leaves

1 cup water

Method

- Rub the fish chunks with salt and ½ teaspoon turmeric powder and keep aside.
- Heat 2 tablespoons mustard oil in a pan, add the fish chunks and shallow-fry the fish, turning sides, till it is golden on both sides. Drain and keep aside.
- Heat the remaining oil in the same pan. Add cloves, cinnamon, cardamoms, bay leaf and cumin seeds and sauté for a minute.
- Add onion paste, ginger paste and tomato paste, mix and sauté till the mixture becomes brown.
- Make a paste with ½ teaspoon turmeric powder, red chilli powder, cumin powder, coriander powder and yogurt. Add this to the pan and sauté on low heat till oil separates from the *masala*. Add cashewnut paste and sauté till oil leaves the sides of the pan.
- Add 1 cup water, salt and sugar and bring the mixture to a boil. Add the fried fish, cover and cook for 3-5 minutes or till the oil separates from the gravy.
- Add *ghee* and *garam masala* powder and mix lightly.
- Garnish with coriander leaves. Serve hot.

Note: *Beating the yogurt well enables it to hold smoothly in the gravy without splitting. This preparation can be done with other fish like rui, katla or bhetki.*

Serves: 3-4 ***Preparation Skill Level: Easy***

Chitol Maacher Muitha

Knife fish dumplings in aromatic gravy

Bengalis from East and West Bengal are always competing with each other in everything from football to food. The little differences in their dialects and cuisines have always been conversation starters. This dish earns brownie points for team East Bengal.

Ingredients

Dumplings (Muitha)

1 cup minced *chitol maach* (knife fish)

1 tablespoon ginger paste

1 tablespoon garlic paste

1 tablespoon green chilli paste

1 medium potato, boiled, peeled and mashed

1 teaspoon roasted cumin powder

Salt to taste

3 tablespoons mustard oil

Gravy

3 tablespoons mustard oil

1 medium potato, cubed

2-3 cloves

1 inch cinnamon stick

2 green cardamoms

1 bay leaf

1 cup onion paste

1 tablespoon ginger-garlic paste

½ teaspoon chilli powder

½ teaspoon turmeric powder

1 teaspoon coriander powder

1 teaspoon cumin powder

1 medium tomato, chopped

Salt to taste

Sugar to taste

½ teaspoon green chilli paste

1 teaspoon *ghee*

½ teaspoon *garam masala* powder

2 tablespoons coriander leaves, chopped

2 cups water

Method

- Mix together minced fish, ginger paste, garlic paste, green chilli paste, mashed potato, cumin powder and salt.
- Boil sufficient water in a deep pan. Dampen your hands, take small amounts of this mixture and shape them into balls.

- Drop the balls in the boiling water and cook for 2-3 minutes or till their colour changes. Drain and keep aside. (Do not over-cook. Over-cooking will make the balls rubbery.)
- Heat mustard oil in a pan, add the balls and shallow-fry till lightly coloured. Drain and keep aside.
- For the gravy, heat mustard oil in a pan. Add potato cubes and shallow-fry till lightly golden. Drain and keep aside.
- In the oil remaining in the pan, add cloves, cinnamon, cardamoms and bay leaf and sauté for 1 minute. Add onion paste and ginger-garlic paste, chilli powder, turmeric, coriander and cumin powders. Sauté till the mixture becomes brown in colour. Add tomato, salt, sugar, green chilli paste and sauté till oil separates.
- Add 2 cups water, and bring the gravy to a boil. Add the fish dumplings and fried potatoes, cover and cook for 2 minutes.
- Sprinkle *ghee* and *garam masala* powder and mix. Garnish with coriander leaves and serve hot.

Serves: 4-6 ***Preparation Skill Level: Difficult***

Shol Mulo

Murrel fish cooked with radish

This is a typical 'Bangal' (inhabitants from East Bengal or Bangladesh) dish. Under the broad spectrum of Bengali cooking, there are some differences in cooking techniques and ingredients between 'Bangal' and 'ghoti' (original inhabitants of West Bengal). I am a ghoti, married to a Bangal; therefore I have adapted and assimilated the cooking nuances of both sides. Among the famous imports from East Bengal to today's West Bengal are the 'Ilish Mach' (Hilsa fish) and 'Shutki Mach' (dried fish). 'Shol Mulo' adds to the kitty box of famous imports.

Ingredients

5-6 murrel (*shol*) fish steaks
1 cup radish cubes
Salt to taste
1 teaspoon turmeric powder
½ cup mustard oil
½ teaspoon cumin seeds
1-2 bay leaves
1 teaspoon chopped ginger
½ cup chopped onion
2 medium tomatoes, chopped
1 teaspoon red chilli powder
1 teaspoon cumin powder
1 teaspoon *garam masala* powder
2½ cups water

Method

- Clean the fish steaks and apply salt and ½ teaspoon turmeric powder.
- Heat oil in a pan, add the fish steaks and shallow-fry, turning sides until evenly golden on both sides. Drain and keep aside on a plate.
- In the oil remaining in the pan add cumin seeds and bay leaves and sauté till the seeds being to change colour. Add radish and sauté for 5-7 minutes. Drain and keep aside in a bowl.
- Grind ginger, onion and tomatoes into a paste. Add ½ teaspoon turmeric powder, chilli powder, cumin powder and ½ cup water and mix well.
- Add this paste to the pan and sauté until the raw smell of the spices disappear. Add 2 cups water, the sautéed radish and salt and mix. Cook the mixture for 5-6 minutes. Add fish and cook till the gravy thickens.
- Remove pan from heat, add *garam masala* powder, mix well and cover the pan. Serve hot.

Serves: 5-6 ***Preparation Skill Level: Easy***

MURGI (Chicken), MANGSHO (Mutton), DEEM (Eggs)

The daily traditional Bengali 'murgi' (chicken) and 'mangsho' (meat) preparations are light, flavourful, and watery gravies but the Mughlai influence makes it rich with a very unique aroma. 'Korma', 'kaliya', and 'dorma' are the typical Muslim cooking terminologies that are part and parcel of Bengali cuisine. 'Deem' or eggs are also part of this sequence of meals, and is not restricted to breakfast, as is popular in the rest of the world.

Mutton Rezala

A rich white mutton gravy preparation

The descendants of Tipu Sultan's immediate family settled around the mosque named after the King, at Tollygunge. The eateries around the mosque began to serve dishes from the family's legacy, of which the 'Rezala' (white korma like dish) was the most favourite. I fondly remember my choto-kaku (uncle) carrying doggy bags of rezala from "Royal" restaurant of Chitpur. The delicious taste of mild, white posto-cashew gravy and the succulent meat lingers on till date.

Ingredients

1 kg mutton, cut into medium pieces

3-inch piece green papaya, made into paste

2 cups yogurt

2 tablespoons vegetable oil

1 teaspoon ginger paste

1 teaspoon garlic paste

½ cup *ghee*

1 bay leaf

2 green cardamoms

1 inch cinnamon

2-3 cloves

2-3 black peppercorns

2-3 white peppercorns

3-4 dried red chillies

1 cup onion paste

2-3 green chillies

4 tablespoon poppy seeds-cashewnut paste

½ cup roundels of onion

Salt to taste

1 teaspoon sugar

1 drop of *mitha attar*

½ teaspoon screwpine water

Few saffron strands soaked in 2 tablespoons warm milk

2 cups water

Method

- Mix mutton pieces with 1 cup yogurt, papaya paste, vegetable oil, ginger paste and garlic paste in a bowl. Keep the bowl in the refrigerator to marinate for 3-5 hours.
- Heat *ghee* in a pan. Add bay leaf, cardamoms, cinnamon, cloves, black peppercorns and white peppercorns and sauté till fragrant. Add red chillies and onion paste, mix and sauté till oil separates.
- Add green chillies, poppy seeds-cashewnuts paste and 1 cup yogurt and mix well.
- Add mutton pieces and mix well. Add 2 cups water, cover and cook for 30 minutes to an hour or till the mutton is done. Add onion roundels, salt and sugar and mix well. Cover and cook for 2-3 minutes.
- Add *mitha attar*, screwpine water and saffron milk and mix well. Serve hot.

Chef's Tips

By substituting chicken for mutton, you can make 'chicken rezala'; by using eggs, it can be 'egg rezala'. All these dishes are as delicious.

Serves: 3-4 ***Preparation Skill Level: Moderate***

Chicken Chaap

Big pieces of chicken cooked in aromatic gravy in Muslim style

'Chaap' happens to be a Bengali-Muslim dish. This is yet another offspring of Bengal's love affair with Awadhi cuisine. I became familiar with 'chaap' when I was in college and went out with friends for an adda (chit-chat). This was also the time when I started adoring the 'rezala' from "Sabir's" and 'biriyani' from "Shiraz". I am still smitten by this Mughlai cuisine that Bengal has adapted.

Ingredients

1 kg chicken, cut into big pieces on the bone

½ cup hung yogurt

1 cup onion paste

1 tablespoon ginger paste

1 tablespoon garlic paste

2 teaspoons red chilli powder

1 teaspoon turmeric powder

½ teaspoon green cardamom powder

¼ teaspoon nutmeg-mace powder

Salt to taste

½ teaspoon black pepper powder

½ cup *ghee*

1 teaspoon sugar

½ cup cashewnuts-melon seeds-poppy seeds paste

5-6 strands of saffron dissolved in 2-4 tablespoons warm milk

Few drops of screwpine water

1 teaspoon *garam masala* powder

Few drops of rose water

Method

- Clean and wash chicken pieces and pat them dry with kitchen cloth.
- Prick the flesh of the chicken all over with a fork. Make slashes in the flesh with a sharp knife to allow the marinade to penetrate.
- Take yogurt in a bowl, add onion paste, ginger paste, garlic paste, red chilli powder, turmeric powder, cardamom powder, nutmeg-mace powder, salt and black pepper powder and whisk well.
- Add chicken pieces and rub in well. Keep the bowl in a refrigerator to marinate for 5-6 hours or overnight.

- Heat *ghee* in a pan, add chicken pieces and sauté on high heat. Add sugar along with the remaining marinade and cook uncovered until oil floats on top.
- Add cashewnuts-melon seeds-poppy seeds paste and saffron milk and mix well. Continue cooking until chicken becomes tender and oil separates.
- Add screwpine water, *garam masala* powder and rose water and mix well.
- Serve hot.

Note: *This dish can also be prepared with mutton.*

Serves: 6-8 ***Preparation Skill Level: Moderate***

Murg Mussalam

Whole roasted chicken

It is a popular Indian non-vegetarian recipe, which uses a combination of minced lamb, eggs and chicken. The preparation involves a lot of hard work and patience. However, the end result is well worth the effort! I always clung on to my Muslim friends so that I could get frequent invitations to their homes to be able to enjoy this delectable dish. I still remember, I used to wait for the invite for Eid celebrations from my friends every year only to savour this grand dish.

Ingredients

800 grams whole chicken

1 tablespoon + 1 teaspoon cumin seeds

2 strands mace

A pinch of nutmeg powder

4 green cardamoms

5 cloves

1 inch cinnamon

2 tablespoons ginger-garlic paste

2 tablespoons onion paste

3 tablespoons oil

1 teaspoon green chilli paste

½ teaspoon red chilli powder

½ teaspoon turmeric powder

3 tablespoons yogurt

Salt to taste

2 tablespoons oil

1 teaspoon cumin seeds

2 bay leaves

2 green chillies

3 large onions, chopped

1 teaspoon *garam masala* powder

Stuffing

3 tablespoons oil

1 cup lamb mince

1 medium onion, finely chopped

1 teaspoon ginger-garlic paste

3 tablespoons tomato purée

2 boiled eggs

½ cup water

Method

- Powder together 1 tablespoon cumin seeds, mace, nutmeg, cardamoms, cloves and cinnamon. Add ginger-garlic paste, onion paste, 1 tablespoon oil, green chilli paste, red chilli powder, turmeric powder, yogurt and salt and mix well.

- Apply this mixture all over the chicken and keep it in a bowl in the refrigerator to marinate overnight.
- To prepare stuffing, heat 3 tablespoons oil in a pan. Add onion, ginger-garlic paste and tomato purée. Mix well and sauté till oil separates. Add mince and sauté till brown.
- Add ½ cup water, cover and cook till mince is cooked. Simmer till all the gravy dries up. Keep aside.
- Stuff mince mixture and boiled eggs into the hollow of the chicken.
- Heat 2 tablespoons oil in another pan, add 1 teaspoon cumin seeds, bay leaves and green chillies and sauté till the seeds begin to crackle. Add onions and sauté for 2 minutes.
- Add the stuffed chicken and sauté for 5 minutes. Add the remaining marinade and mix gently.
- Once the chicken is lightly browned, pour in enough water to cover the chicken and cook until done.
- Alternatively, place the stuffed chicken in a greased baking tray and bake in a preheated oven at 180° C for 45-50 minutes.
- Sprinkle *garam masala* powder and serve hot.

Serves: 3-4 ***Preparation Skill Level: Moderate***

GLOSSARY OF KEY BENGALI TERMS

A Few Terms You Need To Know When You Indulge In Bengali Cooking

Ambal : *A sour dish made either with several vegetables or with fish. The sourness is produced by the addition of tamarind pulp or lemon juice or dehydrated mango.*

Alu-bhathe : *Mashed potatoes, the Bengali way.*

Bata : *Ground on a flattened mortar with a pestle.*

Beguni : *Gram-flour coated eggplant fritters.*

Biriyani : *A fragrant dish made of long-grained aromatic rice combined with beef, mutton, or chicken and a mixture of characteristic spices. Sometimes cooked in sealed containers (dum-biriyani).*

Bhaja : *Anything deep-fried, either by itself or in batter. Normally marination for 'bhaja' is only salt and turmeric powder. It is usually had as a side dish.*

Bhaja moshla : *Roasted cumin and red chilli powder. Used for sprinkling on items like ghugni, alur dom and aamer chutney.*

Bhetki : *Freshwater fish. Used extensively to make fish fry, paturi and jhal.*

Bhapa : *Literally means 'steamed'. Fish or vegetables steamed with oil and spices. A classic steaming technique is to wrap the fish in banana leaf to give it a faint musky, smoky flavour.*

Bhate : *A technique where vegetables or daal are steamed with rice. Boiled, mashed seasoned with mustard oil or ghee and spices.*

Bhuna : *A term of Urdu origin. Meat cooked in spices for a long time without water.*

Bora : *Ground meat or vegetable or lentil croquettes bound together by spices and/or eggs served on its own or in savoury gravy.*

Chaap : *Big pieces of meat cooked with aromatic gravy in Muslim style.*

Chhana : *Home-made paneer or cottage cheese.*

Chingri : *Prawn.*

Chorchori : *Mixed vegetables, slow cooked.*

Chhanchra : *Chhanchra is like chorchori, with fried fish-heads.*

Chechki : *Lightly spiced, stir-fried, tempered with 'panch phoron'.*

Chitol : *Knife fish.*

Cholar daal : *Sweetish preparation of Bengal gram with coconut pieces.*

Cholar daal	:	*Split Bengal gram.*
Chop	:	*Crumb-fried cutlets.*
Chowmein	:	*Stir-fried noodles.*
Chutney	:	*Relish.*
Dalna	:	*Mixed vegetables or eggs, cooked in medium thick gravy seasoned with ground spices, Bengali 'gorom-moshla' and a touch of ghee.*
Daal puri	:	*Lentil stuffed parathas.*
Dam or dum	:	*Vegetables (especially potatoes), meat or rice (biriyanis) cooked slowly in a sealed pot over a low heat.*
Dimer devil	:	*Crumb-fried egg and potato cutlets.*
Ecchor	:	*Jackfruit.*
Doi	:	*Curd/yogurt.*
Doodh	:	*Milk.*
Doodh puli	:	*Jaggery and coconut stuffed dumpling poached in milk sauce.*
Dolma or potoler dolma	:	*Anything stuffed like stuffed potol (pointed gourd).*
Dhoka	:	*Lentil cakes.*
Ghoogni	:	*Spicy yellow peas curry.*
Ghonto	:	*Different vegetables chopped or finely grated and cooked with phoron and ground spices. Non-vegetarian ghontos are also made, with fish or fish heads added to vegetables.*
Gorom moshla	:	*Typical ground spice mix made with cinnamon, cardamoms and cloves in equal portion.*
Jhal	:	*Hot and spicy gravy.*
Jhol	:	*A light, watery everyday curry with or without fish or vegetable.*
Kankra	:	*Crab.*
Kalia	:	*A very rich preparation of fish, meat or vegetables using a lot of oil and ghee with a sauce usually based on ground ginger and onion paste and 'gorom moshla'.*
Kalojire	:	*Kalonji or nigella seeds.*
Kasundi or kashundi	:	*A sharp paste of mustard and raw mango pulp, popular as a dipping sauce in Bengali cuisine.*
Khichuri	:	*Rice cooked with lentils and vegetables.*

Kobiraji cutlet	:	*Cutlet covered in egg net.*
Koi	:	*Sweetwater fish or climbing perch.*
Koraishutir kochuri	:	*Green peas stuffed puri (deep-fried puffed bread).*
Kofta	:	*Ground meat or vegetable croquettes bound together by spices and/or eggs served alone or in savory gravy.*
Korma	:	*Slow cooked with yogurt, cashewnut paste and other spices.*
Labra	:	*Mixed vegetable preparation.*
Lobongo latika	:	*Sweetened stuffed pastry secured with lobongo (clove).*
Langcha	:	*Cylindrical fried dumpling dipped in sugar syrup.*
Luchi	:	*Small round unleavened refined flour bread fried in oil or ghee.*
Maach	:	*Fish.*
Mangsho	:	*Mutton/meat.*
Maan kochu	:	*Taro root stem.*
Malpua	:	*Deep-fried flour batter soaked in sugar syrup.*
Mishri	:	*Sugar candy.*
Mishti doi	:	*Sweetened yogurt.*
Mulo	:	*Raddish.*
Muger daal	:	*Split green gram.*
Musur daal	:	*Split red lentil.*
Motor	:	*Dried white peas.*
Motor daal	:	*Split white peas.*
Mocha	:	*Banana blossoms.*
Momo	:	*Steamed stuffed flour dumplings.*
Mussalam	:	*Whole roasted chicken.*
Nolen gur	:	*Freshly harvested date jaggery.*
Pabda	:	*A freshwater fish. A Bengali favourite.*
Panch phoron	:	*Bengali 5 spice mixture consisting of five spices – (i) cumin seeds (ii) fennel or anise seeds (iii) nigella or onion seeds (iv) fenugreek seeds and (v) radhuni or celery seeds - all mixed in equal proportions. If 'radhuni' is unavailable, replace it with black mustard seeds.*

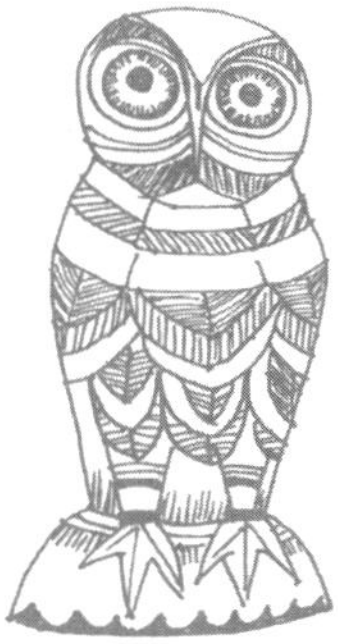

Paturi	:	*Typically made with fish, seasoned with spices (usually shorshe or mustard) wrapped in banana leaves and steamed or roasted over charcoal fire.*
Patishapta	:	*Rolled crêpes with coconut jaggery filling.*
Pish pash	:	*An Anglo-Indian delicacy; a mushy pilaf using meat and milk.*
Pithe	:	*Home style desserts.*
Poroṭa	:	*Bread made from wheat flour and fried in the oven until golden-brown.*
Posto	:	*Poppy seeds.*
Polau	:	*Fragrant dish of rice with ghee, spices and small pieces of vegetables. Long grained aromatic rice is usually used, but some aromatic short grained versions such as Kalijira or Gobindo bhog may also be used.*
Pora	:	*Literally means charred. Vegetables are wrapped in banana leaves and roasted over wood, charcoal or coal fire. Some vegetables with skin such as begun or eggplant, are roasted directly on flame. The roasted vegetable is then mixed with onions, oil and spices.*
Radhaballabi	:	*Spicy urad-daal stuffed fried bread.*
Radhuni	:	*Ajmud or celery seeds. Radhuni is a part of 'Panch phoron'.*
Rezala	:	*A rich white gravy preparation influenced by the Mughals.*
Roll	:	*Kebabs cylindrically wrapped with parathas.*
Rui and katla	:	*Most popular freshwater fish; also known as rohu - belongs to the carp family.*
Ruṭi	:	*Unleavened bread roasted on a tawa and puffed over an open flame.*
Seka	:	*Pan roasted.*
Shingara	:	*Deep-fried stuffed dough pockets.*
Shol	:	*Murrel fish.*
Shorshe	:	*Mustard.*
Shorshe bata	:	*Mustard paste.*
Sondesh	:	*Sweet cottage cheese cubes.*
Thor	:	*Banana stem.*
Torkari	:	*Vegetable curry.*
Urad daal or kolai er daal	:	*White lentil.*